this
way
to the
sea

this way to the sea

THE TRUE STORY OF A NEW LIFE WITH AN OLD LOVE

GILLIAN NICHOLSON

PIER
9

for Christo and Alix

chapter one

'All you need is ignorance and confidence;
then success is sure.'

Mark Twain

It's a warm still evening in early March. Swarms of moths flicker around the veranda lights as Christo and I set up our makeshift picnic on the small square of carpet we've dragged outside. There's a softening Tasmanian camembert in foil wrap, hummus in its plastic container and a box of water crackers.

'Could you turn off the lights, love?' I ask, settling down beside our feast and wishing the moths away as I stare out at the steely ocean. The soft blue sky fading to pink washes warmly over the flat-topped profile of Grassy Head. A crescent moon has risen in the north-east, dangling two stars along with it like some cosmic mobile. Somewhere in the bush surrounding the house two birds call sweetly to each other.

A light sea breeze stirs the tattered leaves of the bananas growing opposite, making a whispering sound like the faint drizzle of rain. And at the end of the veranda our dog has flopped down to hang her head over the edge, ears pricked forward, mesmerised by the antics of some bug or other.

Christo slides open the screen door, and I look up into his lovely face as he hands me a coffee mug filled with sparkling shiraz. There's never been such a husband.

As we sit on the hard floor holding hands like a couple of young lovers, breathing in the peace and quiet all around us, I realise I haven't been this happy in years.

'Well, here we are, babe,' Christo says.

'Here's to us,' I reply, and we clink mugs to toast the moment. We've just become owners of a banana farm.

It's probably the sort of thing you do only once, like throwing in the best job you've ever had to be with the love of your life or buying a sailing boat without knowing the difference between a jib and a mainsail.

But in our case, this isn't the first time we've decided on the path less travelled. Christo, in fact, had left a job he absolutely loved in Brisbane to marry me in 1981. And I had insisted on buying a yacht not long after that because, well ... I fancied sailing on beautiful Sydney Harbour and, besides, it was bright yellow like the Mini Moke we'd just bought as a symbol of our new life together.

Our family, and those who have seen us explore one new passion after another during twenty-two years of marriage, aren't going to be surprised to hear we've bought the farm.

Mum especially. She's the one who taught me the thrill of acting on impulse and grabbing the moment (these days she's calling it synchronicity). There was the day she arrived home with two dozen homeless chirping chicks for my father because he'd vaguely expressed the desire to have chooks (we had no chook house) and another day when she decided to give him two dozen rose bushes (same deal, no garden).

Dad always claimed Mum's spontaneity was one of the reasons he loved her, and Christo claims to feel the same way about me. At least, I take it that's what he means when he says life with me is exciting.

So I call Mum with the news.

'You've bought what, dear?' she asks.

At seventy-nine, she needs to wear hearing aids to be sure of her facts, especially when she's on the phone.

'A farm. A banana farm,' I shout over the piercing whine of the hearing aids being positioned.

'Yes, I can hear you, darling. Why, that ... sounds ... wonderful.' (I believe it could well have been my mother who invented unconditional love.)

'Tell me all about it. How many bananas? Is there a house? Are you going to live there? How exciting! Hang on a minute while I get myself a drink, then you can tell me all about it.' I imagine her at the kitchen sink in her basic box house in Brisbane, pouring a whisky with a splash of tap water, no ice.

'Right,' she says. 'I'm ready.' So I tell her everything.

It begins with a phone call from my sister Janet.

'Hi. It's me. What're you doing?' She sounds excited.

'Nothing much.'

My family — Janet in Kempsey, and Mum and my youngest sister Kathleen in Brisbane — keeps in touch by telephone. It's been a few weeks since I talked to Janet.

'Freelancing is going quite well,' I tell her from my 'office', a 3-metre square cramped alcove off the corridor of our tiny terrace house in Sydney's Bondi Junction. 'Plenty of work at the moment.'

Mostly I've been interviewing local celebrities for *The Australian Women's Weekly*, happy yarns about them falling in love, getting married and having babies. I've also been writing human interest pieces for a couple of the weekly magazines. It's fun to be writing again after more than twenty years as a magazine editor, getting back to the reason I became a journalist in the first place. And the income, although irregular, is extremely welcome; after all, we do have a mortgage … and a teenage daughter.

'Can you get a week off in November?' Janet asks. 'I bought a week's holiday rental in South West Rocks at a charity auction — for you and me. We never spend much time together and when we do all we seem to talk about is our kids.' Which is true. That might be because she has four of them.

I've loved South West Rocks since I came across it around thirty years ago — a spontaneous detour while driving the Pacific Highway between Brisbane and Sydney. Big development on that whole mid-north section of the New South Wales coast is sort of under control and there's an almost anti-progress attitude from the locals that I like. No high rises, no flashy resorts.

Last time Christo and I stayed at the Rocks, in the 1990s, we again fell under its spell and impulsively made a not-very-serious offer for the motel we stayed at. Even then our feelers were out for a change of pace and lifestyle but, as we didn't actually have the necessary $350,000 or any likelihood of getting it, the urge passed. Fortunately. Perhaps something in the eyes of the owners as they trudged from room to room day after day, mop in one hand and toilet cleaner in the other, gave me a glimpse of life as a motelier.

'Just you and Janet. What a nice idea,' Christo says. 'You should go. It'll be fun.' I don't need my arm twisted.

Janet picks me up at Kempsey's big old brick railway station and I notice an Esky in the back of her car, along with a bulging briefcase. 'I'm going to have to come back into town for a couple of meetings, I'm afraid,' she explains. 'But we should have at least four full days together.' Janet is Kempsey's mayor, red robes, rattling heavy chains and all.

Sitting on the balcony in holiday sarongs, we quaff white wine and yarn as we haven't done for a long, long time, talking about the future (not looking particularly wonderful, in financial terms, for either of us), the terrifying speed of life passing us by, the stuff that matters here and now … and, of course, the kids. Hers — Tom, Amy, Liz and Jack — and mine, Alix.

We eat pizza, drink too much and laugh a lot. Separated by seventeen months in age, Janet's the sister I grew up with, loathed for a few teenage years and now count as a close friend. We've shared a lot.

'Guess what?' she asks. Janet loves to spring surprises. 'I've booked us on a fishing charter.'

When we were kids, every holiday was a fishing holiday — clambering in and out of old runabouts with inboard motors, sucking yabbies up out of the sand with a shiny stainless steel pump, untangling fishing lines the wind had tied into frustratingly intricate knots. I haven't been fishing for years.

At five the next morning, we're at a boat shed on the Macleay River, ready to board our craft with three men and a teenager who belongs to one of them.

'Morning everyone,' the skipper, Mark, says brightly. 'Bit rough out there today so we won't be going wide. Still, we should have a good day.'

Out wide? Janet clues me in. On the southern side of the Rocks is Smoky Cape, which scoops out seawards forming a reverse J-shape and provides shelter from the wind. We'll be fishing inside the cape's shadow rather than beyond it.

As Mark and his deckie pass out lifejackets in preparation for crossing the bar, we motor along the breakwater into the dazzling sun. There's a slight swell as we reach the ocean but the weather is lovely. The deckie walks around baiting lines for us, five hooks to a line, and as we come to a stop he explains we're after baitfish — slimy mackerel.

'Just drop the line over, then pull it out.' I do exactly as he tells me, pulling in my line along with five small fish spinning silver in the early light. Swiftly, he and Mark move around the boat slipping the little fish from the hooks before setting the lines again for another cast. Within fifteen minutes we have a bucket full of the sardine-sized tiddlers and Mark turns the boat, searching the depths with his sonar.

'We'll try off Grassy,' he calls to the deckie, who's passing out mugs of instant coffee and freshly made Anzac biscuits — which have a distinct fishy aftertaste — for breakfast. They are delicious.

We anchor off Grassy Head. It doesn't look like much from the boat ... just a small rocky outcrop hardly big enough to interrupt the long sweep of sandy beach, just another unremarkable headland catching the waves. It's not even particularly grassy, although towards its crest there is sparse vegetation.

I see no houses, no shops, no people.

'Is that in your shire?' I ask Janet, dismissing the headland with a glance.

'Only just,' she says. 'The next headland along is Middle Head, then Scott's Head, which is in the Nambucca Shire.'

There's nothing much at Grassy except a caravan park, she explains, although the Macleay River used to run into the sea there until a major flood in 1893 diverted it to the Rocks. All that's left at Grassy is a shallow estuarine backwater that runs from Grassy all the way back to where we boarded this morning.

I weave a slimy mackerel onto my hook and cast with the run of the tide, welcoming the warmth of the sun on my arms and legs. Sydney, the smog and the stress are a seven-hour train ride behind me and, whether we get a fish feed or not, I want to soak up every minute of this day.

Everything is perfect — the grey grittiness under my fingernails, the rich smell of bait on my clothes, my hair matted with sticky salt, the tangy breeze. The hours pass gently with the rocking of the boat and Janet bags two fish. How can something so simple feel so good?

After two or three days of unwinding I'm ready, like every true-blue Sydneysider with (or even without) time on their hands, to indulge in a little window shopping for real estate. I don't actually want to buy anything, but you never know ...

There are plenty of houses for sale at the Rocks but most of them remind me of suburbia — brick veneer, tiled roofs, square lawns, all comfort and no charm. I'm a 'good bones' house buyer, one of the reasons that at our age Christo and I aren't as flush as some of our friends who have put commonsense above falling for renovator's delights.

'What's the next big thing around here? Any areas that haven't been discovered yet?' I've gone into Kempsey to talk to one of the agents my sister has recommended. Paul his name is, and I know straight away I can trust him. His face, or what I can see under a bushy beard, is scored with smile lines and his eyes twinkle. Besides, he's about my age. A definite plus.

'Stuarts Point, probably,' he says, without hesitation. 'In fact, I sold a place on the water at Fisherman's Reach for $87,000 about eighteen months ago, and sold it again for $145,000 just last week.'

My nose for adventure starts to twitch. 'If you have time now, I could show you around,' he says, smiling broadly. Come in, spinner. My sister and I are already climbing into his four-wheel drive.

Paul takes us up the Pacific Highway a bit past the South West Rocks turnoff, then dips into the tiny township of Stuarts Point. We turn right at the shops, past the butcher, newsagent, takeaway and a Four Square store, then along the estuary that Paul says locals still refer to as the river so many decades after the storm of 1893. Five kilometres on, he pulls off the road into the shade of a line of trees on the edge of a tranquil beach. This, he explains, is Fisherman's Reach.

For a few moments we sit enjoying the quiet and peaceful scene. A couple of padlocked timber jetties, rather worse for wear, lurch haphazardly into the shallow waters, bearing warning signs to deter the curious. Oyster beds lap up the rich estuarine soup beyond a boat ramp built next to a big tin shed. A glorious yacht with rust-coloured sails sits at anchor, nose turned into the tide.

'See that shack up there? The one on the narrow block.' Paul hunches over the steering wheel and points through the windscreen to a cluster of weekenders across the road from the river.

'Now I sold that one, as I mentioned, for $87,000. Then I sold it again for almost twice as much as that. All in less than two years.'

A little timber place on the water for $145,000. Hmmm. Judging by the amount of bracken around, I reckon there would be sandflies, but at that price I could afford a cupboard full of repellent.

He starts the car. 'Would you be interested in seeing an 8-hectare farm with fabulous views over Grassy Head? Walking distance to the beach. Good house.'

Does Australia need rain? Christo and I have fantasised about living on what he calls 'an alp overlooking the sea' for most of our married life.

Paul is still talking. 'I need to drop in and say hello to the bloke who's selling the place anyway. He's a real character. Grows the most incredible orchids.'

We drive back through the Point, past the Workers' Club at 50 kilometres per hour, and turn right at the tavern for the 80-kilometres-an-hour stretch to the Grassy Head Reserve.

After a few minutes we turn into a dusty dirt road, coming to a sweet little freshly painted yellow house with a cute picket fence and expansive gardens. I feel a surge of excitement. But that's not it, Paul says.

'That's where the mail's delivered for the people who live up here,' he explains, indicating a row of variously shaped letterboxes.

A little farther on is a grey weatherboard building with a red galvanised iron roof. Real Australian charm. Maybe with a bit of work …

'That's an old dairy,' says Paul.

Oh. Of course.

There we turn onto a private road: down a slope, over a few potholes, through a patch of dense rainforest on the left and farmland on the other side of a barbed wire fence where a family of five wallabies grazes in the tall grass. They lift their heads, watching us for a minute or two before returning to their feed.

We bump over a cattle grid, drive over a rise and the vehicle comes to a stop right beside a giant mango tree, bowed down with ripening fruit.

'This is where the property starts,' Paul says, waving his arm out the window. There's no fence line I can see, just the mango tree, tall grass, bracken and some bushes covered with purple flowers. I think they might be tibouchina, a Brazilian native, but I'm not sure.

'The boundary goes right through the middle of the mango tree.'

I wonder who gets the mangoes?

We get going again, barely slowing as we approach a rustic clapboard building, cobbled together with panelling that's painted pale green. The side facing the road has no wall and, as Paul accelerates past it to take on the sharp grade ahead, I catch sight of a dim interior, three white bathtubs and rough-hewn poles holding a tin roof in place. This can't be it.

'And that's the banana packing shed,' Paul informs us, picking up speed and scattering loose gravel as we climb the short steep hill. I turn around and see, on a roof that's obviously been patched many times over the years, a handpainted sign, 'This way to the sea', and arrows pointing back the way we've come.

Ugh ... ahead of us is a high fence of corrugated green steel, but then we're at the big white house obscured by the fence. This is it.

'How do you like the view?' Paul asks, as we clamber down from the four-wheel drive.

As if he doesn't know. The view is glorious, and all around us — Clydesdales grazing on flat land below, hillsides of tall plantation trees, uninterrupted views of the ocean from north to south and spouts of sea spray smashing against Grassy Head's north face.

My heart is pounding. I'm elated, not just because it's so beautiful but because I sense that this might, just might, be our alp. It's a working farm; bananas grow everywhere I look, probably thousands of them.

Paul leads us to the far side of the house. 'That's national park, right on your western boundary.' *Our* western boundary? 'All of that big hill you can see back there. It used to be a state forest, but the locals lobbied for it to become a national park and got it.

'You've got the park at the back and the ocean in front. If this place were mine,' Paul continues, embracing almost 360 degrees of magic view with a broad sweep of his arm, 'I'd be putting some cottages along the crest of this hill and renting them out. You'd make a killing. This is the best view for miles and miles.'

As he walks up to the house calling to the owner, the memory of a kids' book I loved pops into my head — the story of Johnny 'Appleseed' Chapman, the lone folk hero who planted the American wilderness with apple seeds back in the 1880s. It was illustrated with drawings of a young gap-toothed man wearing a saucepan on his head (I can't recall why), but despite that rather odd image I was inspired. While other girls dreamed of becoming princesses I longed to become another Johnny Appleseed.

By the time I was a teenager I had moved on a bit from wearing a saucepan on my head and was daydreaming about single-handedly rescuing the dry heart of Australia by planting trees to bring the rain and transform the desert into an oasis.

That yearning stirs again now.

From the direction of a large structure up past the garage — a greenhouse, or perhaps it's a shadehouse — hurries a slight, wiry figure who, as he nears, drags off one of his work boots and then the other, with a half-hopping gait. I'm a bit disappointed that the owner's at home; it would have been fun to poke around the place by ourselves. Later I'm glad we came to know Brian, a good-hearted, generous man.

Paul makes the introductions. 'Brian, this is Gillian. She's from Sydney. Janet you know. She's the mayor.'

'And my sister.' I put a little pretend hurt into my tone. As I know from going shopping with her in Woolworths, being with Janet the Mayor tends to relegate you to handmaiden status as she takes urgent calls about sewerage problems on one mobile and Australia Day awards on the other, while chatting with her constituents at the checkout.

'Welcome to Grassy,' Brian says, nodding. 'How are you, Paul?'

Turning to Janet, he says shyly, 'You're certainly shaking things up around here. Mind you, I think we might have needed it.' He bends to tug off his thick socks, stuffing them into his boots, which he arranges tidily at the base of the concrete stairs.

'Please, come up onto the veranda.' Brian rests his tanned forearms on the white steel railing and we line up beside him in the same fashion, facing the ocean and letting the view do its magic.

'You're a little bit late for whales,' Brian says, scanning the horizon just in case. 'They've all made their way back south with their calves by now, but they'll be back in July. We can lose hours sitting here looking out to sea, watching the whales and container ships. You get a pretty good view of the Sydney to Coffs yacht race, too. That's spectacular. At night you'll see the lights of the fishing boats.'

We breathe it all in.

'Come in and have a look at the house,' Paul says.

Brian patters ahead of us, barefoot, and we quickly shuck our shoes, too — the floor inside is highly polished parquetry, and there doesn't seem to be a mark on it.

'The house is almost brand new. Brian built it himself and he did it properly — on brick piers, not a concrete slab. This house will withstand just about anything, from termites to cyclones, won't it Brian? Did you notice underneath the house? Perfectly dry.'

Ah, Christo would be impressed. Almost new, nothing to spend, solid. As houses go, it didn't bowl me over from the outside. Plain and simple, functional, low-maintenance. Again, I thought, this is Christo's idea of a great house.

'And as you can see, it's been cleared all around so bushfires are no threat, and the roof is sloped to collect maximum rain. You'll never run out of water.'

Inside, it's all white walls and timber. Sea-blue tiled floors in the bathrooms — and there are three of them, for heaven's sake, two are ensuites. A study with handmade timber shelving, walls of tongue-and-groove panelling in the dining room, a handcrafted timber mantelpiece above the enclosed wood-burning fire, and a servery made from laminated timbers — lustrous golds, reds and browns. I have no doubt that every square centimetre of this house has been crafted with precision, care and practicality.

But it's the storage that really impresses me. The fuse box is in the broom cupboard, there's a cupboard just inside the door for work boots and hats and, behind another set of doors in the entrance hallway, more shelves … for preserves.

In the laundry we find a cupboard for the large hot water system, a recess high on one wall to accommodate a TV and a built-in ironing board (conveniently located opposite the TV cubicle).

'Would you like to see the orchids now?' Brian asks eagerly.

Months after this visit, Christo and I hear an anecdote about Brian's orchids: the first thing he did when he bought the land twelve years earlier was to build a shadehouse. The house itself came later.

Taking our cues from Brian, we put on our shoes outside and follow him along the concrete path connecting the house to a two-car garage built in matching style. Even the garage has a slim view over Grassy and there's a bonus — another toilet.

Four toilets? Drought?

'You won't have a problem with water,' Brian says reassuringly, his eyes dancing. 'I'll show you the tanks later.'

The garage is roomy enough; Brian's ute takes up one side, the rest is chockers with building materials.

He has an elaborate nursery set-up. On the right, an arched steel-framed structure roofed in green cloth that reminds me of a small Quonset hut or a very poor man's Crystal Palace; it's a good 4 metres high. The floor is made up of long parallel concrete walkways about 30 centimetres wide, with beds of sand between them. Steel framework along one wall suggests that there were benches here for plants, but the building is otherwise empty and I am too polite to ask questions. After all, we're taking up Brian's time … and we're not serious buyers.

Slung across the greenhouse just above head height is a thick rope. Brian catches my eye, smiling. 'That's where I hang my washing if it's raining. Gets very warm in here.'

The greenhouse is separated from a similarly sized shadehouse by a covered walkway, and inside the shadehouse is another, smaller one, with its own air-conditioner humming away!

'It's too warm at Grassy for the orchids I want to grow,' Brian explains. 'That's why I'm going to Dorrigo. It's higher country and much cooler.'

He takes us into the igloo to see his orchids, just a fraction of the collection, he says.

I know a basic cymbidium when I see one, but there's not one orchid here I recognise. A couple are in flower though, displaying tiny buds of bright yellow and white. Another has a long trailing stem dotted with lacy-edged purplish flowers and a spicy perfume.

'You could start your own nursery business here,' Paul says. 'All the hard work's been done.'

Funny, I've heard that line about hard work from city real estate agents from time to time, too.

But I suppose he's right. I could. Can't be too hard to raise plants, and everything is here. There are several benches built into the shadehouse; they won't be going anywhere. And a fertiliser tank, though I have no idea how that works.

My imagination is working like blazes. We're intelligent people. We could make this work — what with the bananas and this nursery, surely we could make a living of sorts.

I see us eating home-grown tomatoes all year round, supplying local restaurants with seven varieties of lettuce, even growing orchids ourselves for the Sydney market ...

That yearning suddenly overwhelms me and I turn to Janet.

'I would give anything to live here. I've never felt so strongly about anything in my life.'

'Call Christo,' says my sister.

'To tell him what? We can't afford this …'

'Call him anyway.'

So I call him and try to explain. I realise I am shaking with excitement.

'I've found this place for sale, darling. A farm. The house is sturdy and new, and the views are unbelievable. Yes, exactly. An alp overlooking the sea. Eight hectares. I know it's crazy to even contemplate it, but … '

Christo simply says: 'Call the bank.'

'But you haven't even seen it.'

'Just call them.'

And that's the day we bought the farm.

chapter two

'I realized that all the really good ideas
I'd ever had came to me while I was
milking a cow. So I went back to Iowa.'

US 'regionalist' artist Grant Wood

'You know that you're doing something we all want to do?' says our friend Bruce. We're at his fifty-something birthday party two days after Christmas.

It's a muggy Sydney night in an immaculate North Shore courtyard garden, people jamming in between the manicured *Buxus* and the soothing water feature.

'It's great news. Good move. Wish we had the courage to get out of Sydney.' There's a genuine grin on his face and a longing look in his eyes.

Christo and I can only beam back. It's funny, I've met so many people over the years who did the sea change thing before it was fashionable and always wondered how they had found the confidence to leave the city for the unknown — and admired them for it. Now it's us.

Bruce calls over some of his other guests to inspect photos of the property, which I'd printed out from the real estate agent's website and folded into my bag (after cutting out the asking price! I wasn't entirely ready to share).

'Meet Gillian and Christo. Guess what these two have just done?' he says.

Tonight is the first time we've gone public with the news, and we're a surprisingly serious hit at the party. Everyone wants to know where our farm is (400 kilometres north of Sydney), how big it is (8 hectares), when we are moving (probably in twelve months) and what we plan to do there.

It's a leap of faith, I tell them. Maybe we'll farm the bananas ourselves, or maybe we'll plant organic bush tucker — that appeals to me. Organics are big business, I've heard, and I've seen bush tucker on city menus.

Maybe we'll build a B&B cottage for travellers, and share our fabulous views. ('Did we mention that the house is on a ridge overlooking the ocean?')

Farm forestry has a responsible green ring to it, too. One of our Grassy Head neighbours has grown a whole hillside of native trees for cabinet timber. Of course allowing twenty-five years for the natives to reach maturity, if we did that we wouldn't live long enough to harvest them, but what the heck.

I'd like some farm animals to keep the grass down and enrich the soil but, although Christo says he wouldn't mind a few alpacas and chooks, he's firmly against goats (they smell and escape all the time), cows (no fencing, no cattle grid), donkeys (stupid things!), geese (noisy and messy) and ducks (messier than geese).

We haven't done a budget or even properly considered how we're going to get by financially. One party guest who's been digging for the hows, wheres and whys of our sea change, comments, 'If you budgeted for it, you probably wouldn't do it.'

He could be right.

When we go to see our city lawyer, he wants to focus on how we're going to make a living too.

'Hmm … 7.2 hectares of the property is under bananas. You know how to farm bananas, do you?' he asks, his Parker pen hovering over the title deed.

'It's not a problem,' I say. 'There's a tenant farmer.'

I have already researched tenant farming on the internet and found there are a couple of different ways to handle the relationship. I found a website of arcane publications specialising in farming matters, from how to fence a pastoral property dam to recognising common weeds, and bought a book about tenant farming which I read, picking through the tables of budgets and variables for a glimmer of understanding.

So I believe I'm on firm ground with this issue. Does a city lawyer know anything about the working relationship between landholder and tenant farmer?

He lifts his eyes from the contract and stares through neat rimless spectacles. I think I detect a hint of amusement in his eyes.

'Annual rent reviews? Liability insurance? Maintenance of equipment? GST? Notice to vacate?'

'The young farmer's a nice bloke,' I say. Christo hasn't met Greg yet, but I've said g'day to him a couple of times and he's given me a friendly wave from his truck. 'We'll sort something out. We don't want to get all legal and complicated.'

I drop our photos on the desk so the solicitor will understand our rationale for buying the farm. 'This is it. See the views?'

'Yes. Lovely up that way,' he says dismissively.

But he doesn't see the surf spurting spume up the side of Grassy Head, he doesn't hear wind wheezing through the gums, he doesn't feel the tingle of anticipation.

'Is your property fenced?'

'Mmmm ... not sure,' I reply.

'Fencing is very, very expensive. You might want to negotiate the price down if it's not fenced. How big is your water tank?'

'Twenty-five thousand gallons.'

Got him on that one!

'And this private road ... '

Our house is at the end of a bumpy 1.5 kilometre private road, hedged by wattles and rainforest trees and prone to potholes after rain.

'... it's a right of way. Are you aware of the maintenance issues?'

'Umm ...'

So many questions. I squeeze Christo's hand, totally confident. 'We'll work it out, won't we, love?'

Three months later it's official; the bank has bought itself a farm at Grassy and we now have a mortgage of just under $1 million.

'Say it quickly,' I tell friends, 'and it doesn't sound too bad.

She'll be right.' And I truly am unconcerned. I believe with all my heart in our future here; it will be wonderful.

'If it all goes to hell in a handcart,' Christo adds, pulling out one of his favourite expressions, 'we'll sell our house in the city.'

Our plan is to rent out the farm and stay in Sydney while our daughter gets settled into uni and we prepare to move to the farm permanently in a couple of years. We're going to have to save, but first we need to buy a four-wheel drive vehicle for our trips to Grassy. Our old Magna won't cope with the private road, much less the rough tracks through the bananas. Besides, Alix is learning to drive and will try to claim the Magna soon.

A second-hand Subaru Forester is our first choice, the car recommended by two friends, one of whom lives in the country.

'When did you want the vehicle?' asks the salesman at the inner city car yard. We're in a hurry. Settlement is approaching.

'Well, all I have is this one — it's a 1997 model.' The age of the car and the price he quotes don't interest us. 'Good Foresters are rare as hen's teeth and not cheap, you know. They have one of the highest resale values on the market.'

Up the road is a flashy Honda dealer. Well, why not a Honda — a CRV? A neatly suited young man takes us through the benefits of a sparkling run-out model, four-wheel drive of course, that's on special. It has all the mod cons too. CD player, power windows. I can't think of one good reason not to buy it. Looks good to me.

He shows us the pièce de résistance, tucked away under the floor mat in the back — a fold-up picnic table. How lovely. And the price is not much more than the second-hand Forester, considering that it is brand spanking new.

'Let's give Bear a call,' Christo suggests quietly. Bear is Alan's nickname; he's a good mate who really knows cars.

'Nah,' he responds to my call. 'Nice car, but you want something with more grunt.' Even the cute fold-up picnic table won't bring him around, so we move on to the nearby Holden dealer where there are plenty of second-hand cars, not all of them Holdens.

There we find the vehicle for us — a Toyota Prado, gleaming white on the tarmac with showroom magnetism. A salesman is quickly at our side, shading himself from the sun in the kind of white hat you see on Warnie when it's Glenn McGrath's over.

'Like to take her for a drive, mate?'

Christo appears to be considering, but it's for show. 'Yeah, all right, mate.' And the two buddies set off.

The Prado is a helluva lot dearer than the Forester and it's all happening so fast, I reckon it's time to phone our friend again.

'Bear? Hi. We're looking at a 2001 Prado.'

'That's more like it. How much on the clock? Hang on I'll get it up on the internet. Which dealer is it?' Tap, tap, tap.

'Looks like a good buy. When Christo gets back, run the air-conditioning really hard. If there's a lot of dust, it means it's been off road a lot and you need to ask more questions. Otherwise, go for it.'

The boys get back. 'Come inside where it's cool,' I hear the salesman tell Christo, 'and we'll go through the paperwork.' Finance? No problem.

The Nicholsons have a farm vehicle.

Settlement day. Christo has taken a week off work so we can drive up to the property to meet Brian for the handover. In the back of the truck: two borrowed foam mattresses with torn floral covers and Bindi, our gorgeous, crazy, black-and-tan Airedale terrier.

We pull up outside the house where Brian's waiting beside his ute, the trailer packed with tools, an Esky and a stack of timber tied down with rope.

Leaping from our car, Bindi almost bowls Brian over, then executes an ungainly aerial pirouette and tears off into the tall grass. The pure-bred Airedale from the rolling lowlands of eastern Victoria has found heaven.

We've arrived a bit later than arranged and Brian's keen to be off, but first, 'Just a couple of things to show you before I go,' he tells Christo, leading us past the greenhouse to two extra water tanks behind the potting shed. One is a back-up for the main tank (10,000 gallons), he says, the other a fertiliser tank (5000 gallons) and, on the ground between them, a network of white plastic pipes and large red and blue taps.

Brian explains, 'To use the fertiliser tank, turn this blue cock clockwise and that red cock this way but,' darting into the igloo, 'turn this tap on first. See.' Hang on, the blue then the red …

Christo is nodding, so he must have it.

'Now the house pump,' Brian rushes around to the back of the garage. 'You need to change the filter every six months or so. I've left you a spare one in the garage.' He lifts the top off a dog kennel-sized housing made of the same corrugated steel used along the top of the driveway, and the two men peer inside.

'Maybe you'd better write this down,' Brian suggests. I race back to the vehicle for a pen and scrap of paper. I don't know what happens if you don't change a pump filter every six months, but Brian is taking the lesson very seriously and Christo is concentrating hard. I take notes. I must put this piece of paper somewhere safe.

'I think you'll be right,' Brian says back at the ute, producing three tinnies. 'Oh, I've left you a few orchids and there's a pot with a big cycad in it. You can have it if you like.'

It's a warm day and the beer disappears quickly. No worries, I think, wondering what Christo's feeling right now.

We wave Brian off as he chugs down the hill, creating a dusty wake. We're alone at last. Grassy is ours.

Bindi's vanished, so Christo gives her a whistle. We hear her crashing through the bush before we see her parting a sea of tall grass as she runs to us. She throws herself onto the lawn at our feet, grunting and rolling and wiping her head with one paw, her beard matted thickly with black cobbler's pegs. Other people call them farmer's friends, but I remember them from my childhood as cobbler's pegs, the little black spikes clinging to my clothes any time I played in the bush around our Brisbane home.

I don't have a brush to groom Bindi; her curls will have to stay weed-thatched until we go back to Sydney. I don't think she's the least bit bothered.

That night, out on the veranda, we sip red wine and listen to CDs on an old sound system, an ex-rental Christo bought from a shop in Sydney. He can't last a day without music.

We hit the thin foam mattresses to the velvet crooning of the Mills Brothers singing 'Lazy Bones', not to sleep but to wonder at this amazing thing we've done. Our bedroom faces the sea and is so high it seems we're floating in the clouds.

A big storm is breaking on the horizon, bolts of jagged electricity occasionally spearing the sea while sheet lightning dazzles the sky all the way from the Rocks to Nambucca. Thunder rolls around us, bringing Bindi to her feet on the veranda outside our bedroom, tail wagging with excitement. Warm under the sleeping bag, snuggled up to Christo, I'm awash with happiness and optimism.

The storm rumbles on all night, waking us from time to time, but never disturbing the spell. Morning is just as magical, dawn breaking suddenly across the now tranquil sea, sunlight flooding our uncurtained bedroom and blinding us with molten silver.

What a way to wake up. From our spot on the floor, the view is breathtaking: shimmering ocean and hills of green. The call of a whip bird slices through the silence, and then a kookaburra begins to laugh and sets off a raucous, happy throng.

'Listen,' says Christo, as the din subsides. He gets up and opens the sliding glass doors to the veranda, where a sleepy dog greets him with a yawn.

I grab my glasses from the floor and follow. 'What?'

'That bird. Can you hear it?'

I *can* hear it: it sounds like a flute. 'Yes. It's beautiful.'

'But can you hear the tune it's singing? It's the theme from *Raiders of the Lost Ark*. Listen,' and he hums along with the bird.

I close my eyes and concentrate on the bird's song. I think I can hear the *Raiders* tune but …

'It's that magpie,' Christo whispers, pointing to the top of the nearest mango tree, and we creep to the edge of the veranda.

'So it is,' I whisper back. Its open beak thrust to the sky, the small black-and-white bird reprises the lilting melody, and I'm half-convinced Christo is right.

'Let's go back to bed, love,' I say, taking his hand.

We spend the morning drifting in and out of sleep, bathed in a light that changes from silver to gold and then orangey pink. I'm feeling unbelievably wealthy today.

Our house stands on a long, grassy strip of land where Brian once grew magnificent heliconia. The area is bare now except for a mango tree at either end, just the right spot for playing *pétanque*. I picture us sitting in the shade of the mango trees, catching sea breezes and sipping Campari and soda as we take turns to toss the silver balls.

Beyond the far mango tree, only just visible from the veranda, is a small corrugated iron shed. I have plans for that too. Chooks. Bindi will keep the foxes away and we will have plenty of fresh, organically produced eggs. (There will be no poison used on our farm, of course.)

We're dying to show off the property. Two days after we arrive, Mum's due to drive down from Brisbane and we've also invited our friend Ian, a mate from Melbourne. Ian knows a lot about running a farm, having grown up in the Victorian countryside with a dad who loved to grow things, and having farmed in Tasmania himself.

Flowers don't interest him much, but he's managed to feed his own family from backyard garden plots for years and has even written a book about it all, with heaps of ideas on everything from raising seeds and DIY hydroponics to backyard irrigation and … chooks. Ian is dead keen to see the place and we're dead keen to get his input. We dub him 'The Mentor'.

He arrives the next morning, fully prepared for roughing it, because we've told him there's no furniture in the house apart from our mattresses, the sound system and a few bits to cook with.

'This is a bit of all right,' he says in greeting, hands on hips and turning to enjoy the view. He unloads the car with vigour and smartly assembles a stretcher bed in one of the bedrooms. Then he unfolds a picnic table with built-in bench seats in our lounge room, sets up a camp stove in our kitchen 'just in case' and pulls a video camera out of his travel kit.

'What a truly lovely spot,' he says, plonking on the safari hat he likes to wear (and I have admired so much in the past that Christo has bought me one for Grassy). 'Let's have a cuppa, then you can show me around.'

We're limited to regular tea bags, but Ian — always ready for anything and everything — extracts from a well-organised milk crate a container offering several tea varieties. He chooses Lapsang Souchong.

It's been a humid morning, with a fine mist hanging tentatively in the gullies and low spots below the house. Now it's drizzling, but the rain is warm and not unpleasant so we decide to chance a walk around the property. Ian puts on a jacket to protect the video camera.

Since Ian has already driven along our southern boundary, we head down the other side of the hill towards Yarrahapinni National Park. It's our first time going around on foot.

Strewn with large rocks and rutted by the heavy rains of many summers, the track isn't easy to negotiate. We pick our way down the hill between a straggling barbed wire fence that sags between old timber posts and neat rows of bananas as far as the eye can see.

'Hang on. First shot,' Ian says, removing the video camera from under his jacket. 'The rain's holding off. I want to get you over near the bananas there.'

Several of the bananas have long plastic bags of different colours draped over their bunches of unripe fruit.

'What's the significance of the colours?' Ian asks.

I have no idea. With a shrug, I move into shot and pick up a longish stick so I can lift the skirt of one of the bags and peer up into it without getting too close to what might be in there with the bananas. I prod around hesitantly.

'Got to be careful of snakes in bananas. Green snakes. They won't kill you but they can give you a nasty bite.' It's not the answer to his question but it's one of the few things I do know about bananas, having been raised in Queensland.

So Ian answers his own question. 'Different colours for different maturing times, I reckon.'

Bindi has run off somewhere through the grass and, although we can hear her thrashing around somewhere below, she doesn't come to our calls. The infamous Airedale stubbornness.

Suddenly there's an angry quacking followed by a huge splash, and we see four ducks take flight above the dam. Within minutes, a wet and muddy dog is back with us, curly hair flattened against her panting body and full of grass seed, and on her face the biggest grin a dog can do.

Christo is hacking helpfully at tall stands of bamboo that are blocking our way, using a cane knife. He loves guy tools. This one he bought yesterday from The Trading Post, an odd little store in Macksville that sells camping and fishing gear, as well as broken radios and old things that all look partly deconstructed to me.

'It's cow cane, not bamboo, I think you'll find,' says our knowledgeable friend, striding ahead of us. Christo gives the clump a few whacks anyway, and strips the leaves from three of the canes to create staffs for us all. Ian tests his with a swift jab into the red soil, but it bends under the pressure so he heaves it. I keep mine, though, and so does Christo. Solidarity forever.

Breaking through the stands of cow cane, we come to the dams, both of them, according to the real estate agent, are spring-fed. They look more like lakes than dams, almost landscaped, bounded on the far side by a high wall of red earth, and merging into a grassy bog close to where we're standing. And they're swimming with water lilies. In the dam nearer us is a children's slippery dip. The beauty of the dams and, even more so, their functionality, impresses Ian.

'Ah, I see you have a reliable water supply.'

'Well,' I tell him, feeling almost apologetic, 'the dams aren't actually ours. They belong to our neighbour, Mark. We don't have any *real* dams … just one near the mango tree as you come onto our property, and it's only half ours.'

He gives me a look that plainly asks the question: why would you buy a farm without water?

The answer is, it didn't occur to us.

'So how does this young tenant farmer get the water to his irrigation lines?'

'There's a pump down here somewhere,' I reply, pointing vaguely to the bush below us. 'Mark lets us use the water in his dams. He's very nice.'

'Hmmm. What sort of pump do you have? Is it in good order?'

'Um, Greg says it's okay but it needs ... um, bleeding? We haven't really looked into it yet.'

Embarrassed by Ian's questions and my ignorance, when I see Christo chopping through the jungle ahead I seize the opportunity to distract Ian from the shortfall in my farming knowledge.

'Look, where Christo is, the Christmas bush. There's quite a lot of them. Hundreds, I reckon.'

'Christmas bush? What's that?'

Christo stops swinging the cane knife and turns around, catching his breath. 'It's a native, mate,' he says. 'Blooms at Christmas time.'

'Greg planted them,' I add. 'He wasn't happy with the harvest last year, but apparently some growers were getting 11 cents a stem for Christmas bush a couple of years ago.'

Ian isn't exactly overawed by its straggly appearance, but he crouches down and films a couple of bushes for the record. The tour continues around the outer edge of the farm, past a scattering of wattles, thickets of noxious lantana and the shrubby tree with the purple flowers that Christo believes is tobacco bush, a weed. Ian agrees. So much for my tibouchina theory.

Climbing back up to the crest at our northern boundary, we show Ian where we will put up a couple of self-contained cabins for tourists ... maybe. But after a few minutes, the mozzies send us back towards the house along another rough track made slippery in the rain, and there are more discoveries: a loquat tree and more mangoes. They're everywhere.

We approach the house just as it starts to bucket down. Bindi's in the home orchard, where Brian has planted mandarin, lemon, orange and lemonade trees and — we think — lychees.

'You've got a couple of stone fruits there, too,' Ian says. 'Could be a peach, maybe a nectarine. Hope you don't get fruit fly here.'

Our mad dog is scrounging around under the macadamia tree for fallen nuts, tossing them one by one into the air as if she's playing jacks, then cracking them with her teeth to get at the sweetness inside.

'You've done good,' Ian tells us with a grin. 'This is a wonderful set-up. I reckon the shadehouse and the greenhouse can make you some money if that's the way you decide to go. But I don't think I can be much help to you with what you can grow here. Remember, I'm a cold-climate man, and this tropical stuff is a bit of a mystery to me.

'Stick to good organic farming principles if you're going to give this a go. And get your infrastructure right. You'll be okay.'

Infrastructure. Got it. But it's Greg's land at the moment.

'I have one question, though. Can you show me how to eat a mango?'

Mum has arrived while we were on tour and stands on the veranda, whisky in hand. 'Hello there,' she calls. 'Look at you, you're all soaking wet. Come in and have a drink.'

Ian joins her as I turn to look at my husband, a pathetic spear of frayed, bendy cow cane in his hand. Mine isn't much better.

'You know what? You two look like that painting, you know, with the man and woman on the farm in the American Midwest. They're standing side by side looking grim ... What's it called? Something Gothic ... yes, *American Gothic*.'

Ian's laughing beside her, lifting his video camera and pointing it in our direction.

'You've got it, Norma.'

We stand straight-faced, hair plastered against our heads, rain dripping into our muddy runners, and pose stiffly.

This is bliss — Grassy Head Gothic.

chapter three

'I got the mid coast blues, I got the mid coast blues
Got mountains to dream on
Beaches to cruise
Oh, Lord, I got the missin' the mid coast blues.'

'The Mid Coast Blues'
by C. Nicholson

At Grassy Head Beach, tides come and go, scooping and shaping hills of sand. Locals congregate early in the morning to assess swell and weather, wet-suited schoolboys hugging surfboards hurl themselves from the rocks in the afternoon, and fishermen cast their hopes into secret bounty holes beyond the breakers as ebb and flow dictate.

Travellers appear at all times of day, tired of the highway, slowing their vehicles to 15 kilometres an hour as they turn into Grassy Head Reserve to choose a shady spot among the coastal banksias, sprawling old figs and sturdy paperbarks in the dune-side caravan park.

Unloading dinghies and surfboards from roof racks, assembling instant tables and chairs and setting their Eskies in a sheltered spot, they revive in the peace and quiet with a cuppa before erecting tents.

The beach awaits, up and over the dunes past the sign declaring 'No dogs' and a blackboard that tells of surf conditions and, sometimes, an upcoming meeting date for the Dunecare group … but not the spot where nude bathers indulge in sun worship, a good kilometre up the beach.

During Christmas and Easter holidays, apparently, there are enough holidaymakers to entice lifesavers to keep watch from their temporary patrol post, a small dome-shaped tent of red and gold plopped at the southern end of Grassy.

But holidays aside, all the real action around here is at the local village of Stuarts Point, back down Grassy Head Road. The Point has a reputation of sorts. Some call it Stupid's Point, while another story they tell is that Stuarts Point isn't the end of the earth, but you can see it from there. I can't see a lot wrong with that myself.

We like what we discover about it in our first week. A tidy town with broad, level streets, where you can dawdle four abreast along grassy footpaths cushioned by sand. Houses old and new, tacked together and project-style — fibro, weatherboard and brick — sport gardens of showy semi-tropical plants.

The cluster of shops is the neighbourhood gathering point: the butcher runs a footy-tipping competition; the post office is closeted inside the takeaway shop; outside the Four Square store the name of someone having a birthday is chalked onto a large blackboard; the hairdressing salon opens four days a week; a community house in a rented cottage offers second-hand items for sale, and comfort and advice free; and, on prime waterfront land, with its back to the river, is a nondescript hall encompassing a small library.

'Let's go for a walk,' I call to Bindi, and she bolts over to Christo, who's standing at the truck flourishing her blue lead so she'll know she's not being conned. Bindi hates car travel and this is not a teasing matter. Never say 'walk' to this dog if you don't mean it, unless you can cope with sad eyes.

We're off to see what's on the other side of the river at Stuarts Point and, by the time we get to the picnic ground adjacent to the caravan park, Bindi's trembling with anticipation, her curved tail rigid as a plaited leather whip handle. Christo snatches up her lead before she can jump down and invade someone's tent or invite herself to a barbecue — a habit she picked up on walks in Sydney's Centennial Park — and strolls towards the sandy beach.

At the water's edge, a man in a beaten-up Akubra leans over a concrete slab on wooden piers cleaning fish, flicking the innards to a flotilla of patient pelicans, then scraping at the sparkling scales. The flakes fly into the air and catch the sun's glint.

'What'd you get?' I ask, walking up to him. Christo would never be so bold.

'Sole and a couple of black fish,' he responds, brushing away bush flies with the scaling tool. 'Not a lot around since the rain. Few mantas over there.' He nods sideways to a picturesque old white wooden footbridge that crosses the river crookedly on sturdy concrete pylons.

It's almost low tide, revealing sandbanks pocked with hundreds of perfect little balls disgorged by blue soldier crabs as they burrowed to safety. Here and there are warm puddles and child-sized lagoons. Gleeful toddlers with brightly coloured buckets and spades chase schools of darting fish and tumble in the shallows.

On the bridge, three Koori kids are fishing with hand lines, using rolled balls of dough as bait. They know to position themselves over the channel, where the deep green waters hold the promise of a big one.

'Jag him, jag him,' yells one of the boys, racing to his mate's side to find the hook is empty. He shakes his head in disbelief.

'Jag him,' a little girl in a red dress echoes, and the disappointed boy moulds more dough onto the small hook.

As we approach the children, I peer into their battered bucket to see a sizeable bream swimming around, its shiny body at an odd tilt. Dinner for one.

Bindi's not enjoying the walk over the bridge at all, unnerved by its sway and the sight of water through the wooden planks, and hauls on her lead until she and Christo reach the mangroves and solid ground.

Here, dogs are allowed to run without leads and she's off, stopping occasionally to explore trails that branch off to the deserted tree-fringed beaches or waterlogged salt marshes where animals, probably wallabies, have crushed a path through broad stretches of spiky dark green reeds. So many sights, so many smells, so many sounds.

The track rises and broadens to an avenue of banksias, Snugglepot and Cuddlepie territory, where the many eyes of May Gibbs's banksia men stare sightlessly as we pass.

We reach the end of the track at the base of a sand dune, the boom of the surf urging us on. Bindi gallops to the top, Christo strides and I trudge behind. One ordinary dune and my legs are feeling the effort. How could I be so unfit? Ah, yes. I've been sitting at a desk for forty years.

So I pace myself up and over. I'm silently trying to catch my breath, pretending to take in the endless view of ocean and appear unaffected by the climb, when I hear Christo calling the dog.

'Did you see where she went?'

There's not a living thing visible in either direction but he whistles anyway against the sting of the sandy wind and the crash of the surf on its outward run. As we walk and call and squint through the haze of sea spray, there is no sign of black and tan.

'Look. There. Quick,' Christo calls, pointing up to the dunes behind us and I glimpse a kangaroo in mid-air, silhouetted against the sky … and, seconds later, our manic dog galloping across the top of the dunes in pursuit.

'Bloody dog,' Christo curses. 'Bindi-i-i-i … ' But Bindi is in another place.

So we wait and walk and whistle. Twenty minutes' later, Christo is still fuming as the two of us set off back to the car, reasoning she will eventually find us. 'That's the last time we bring the dog here without a lead,' he grumps.

'She's just excited, darling, 'I reply. I thought it was funny. 'Don't worry, she'll find us. Let's get a cold drink and wait.'

But he's not to be soothed as he props himself up against the car.

At last we see her tearing frantically up the long beach on the other side of the river, head turning this way and that as she searches for us. There's no way she can see or hear us, but I wave and call anyway. She looks desperate, jumping over fallen trees, nosing around the mangroves and eventually finding the bridge.

And there she stands, out of puff, her sides heaving with exertion and too frightened to cross over alone.

Christo goes to fetch her, the lead in his hand and anger in his step. But Bindi wags her tail as he reaches her, smiles up gratefully and melts his heart all over again.

Christo's started writing songs again. He sits on the veranda floor up against the wall, picking on his prized Gibson as gentle rain starts to fall. There is no wind, and the rain has silenced birds and insects and muted the colours around us — except for the striking, vivid orange blossoms of an enormous African tulip tree just outside the back door. I've only ever seen one of these before, in a natural history documentary. It's so spectacular, so unusual, it almost needs a giraffe standing beneath it, chewing the leaves to complete the impact it makes.

'Hey, babe,' Christo calls, 'I think I've got the makings of quite a nice little blues here, if you'd like to hear it.'

I settle down on the floor a few metres away. 'Yes, please.'

It's been so long since I've heard him play. So much has been in the way, the usual stuff of life. Work, parenthood, bills and, last year, a mild stroke.

Christo's specialist says he has recovered completely, but we both know it could happen again at any time: it's in his genes. Maybe Alix's, too. The possibility hovers, ever present.

I'm sittin' in the city 'n' havin' no fun
Longin' for my little place in the sun
It's not too near 'n' not too far
It's about halfway from where you are

Just a little place but I dig it the most
Away up there on the mid-north coast.
I got the mid coast blues, I got the mid coast blues
Got mountains to dream on
Beaches to cruise
Oh, Lord, I got the missin' the mid coast blues.

He's going back to Sydney tomorrow, Sunday, but I'm staying for a while. Because it's our last day together, we decide to check out our local watering hole, a new-looking tavern that's set back off Ocean Avenue where it meets Grassy Head Road.

The tavern occupies most of a low brick building that also houses a hardware store and real estate agent. Inside, the exposed brick walls make it seem quite gloomy so, while Christo orders a beer for him and a cider for me, I move out the back to the beer garden. This is more like it: outdoor tables with built-in bench seating under shade cloth, a barbecue area and views — across the steel fence — of bushland stirring with birdlife.

Two of the four tables are already taken by drinkers who, for some reason, are wearing funny hats and laughing at each other a lot. Well, it is late on Saturday afternoon. I wonder if, down the track, these people will become our friends.

The frivolity rubs off on us and we relax into the autumn warmth, the refreshing iciness of our drinks and the shriek of sleek red-and-green king parrots swooping recklessly through the trees.

But there's more remarkable entertainment to come. Just past the barbecue area, a fat goanna that must be easily 2 metres long waddles past the pub's patrons checking for scraps of food with its flicking tongue.

It's not the least disturbed by the rowdy lot in silly hats, who don't pay it any attention either. Obviously the lizard is a regular too.

For us, however, all the excitement calls for another round of drinks as we make a toast: 'To our local.'

Christo leaves it until noon before driving back to Sydney, making the most of every minute. He has to be back at work the next day.

'Please take it easy on the road,' I tell him. He loves to drive, to push the speed limit. It's one of the few things we ever argue about, and I worry more since the stroke.

Not too many people know about it; it was not a piece of news we shared with anyone other than close friends and family at the time. You daren't show any sign of weakness in the workplace when you're over fifty.

But Christo's more concerned about me being alone here. 'Will you be okay here without the truck till I get back?' he asks. 'There's still time to get the train from Macksville if you run me in to town now.'

His eyes can't hide how he feels about that alternative. We haven't done the Macksville-Sydney train trip, but Kempsey-Sydney is much the same, just half an hour shorter. The trip is interesting the first time, pleasantly familiar the second and a long drag after that. But it is cheaper than flying or the price of a full tank of petrol.

'I'll be fine, love, don't worry. Let me know when you get there.'

As a matter of fact I actually love the idea of staying put and having Grassy all to myself. Sequestered. I don't need the truck, or television, or human company. I have Bindi and my laptop.

Besides, the last mangoes are ready and waiting …

We've decided I should hang around here for a couple of weeks to sort things out, but it's really no sacrifice. I have my survival rations: the new Janet Evanovich mystery, my

Beethoven string quartets and the Amazing Rhythm Aces CD, the metal wind chimes Christo and I bought when we lived in Auckland, my collection of recipes saved over the years (most untried yet) and Esther Deans' gardening book: *Growing Without Digging.* I'll have plenty to do.

The dawn is spectacular this morning. Out to sea, a line of puffy clouds etched in gold stretches right across the horizon and the sunrise hues of pink and grey melt away under the sun's onslaught. White brilliance strikes through my window, dazzling me awake. It's going to be a glorious autumn day.

My eyes are blurred with sleep, so I allow myself to lie there and savour the stillness. All is quiet except for the constant boom of the surf.

I plan to prune the lemon tree today, a job that's been on my mind since we liberated it from a tree guard last time we were here. It will do better if it's cut back; at least that's what I've learned from my faithful old gardening book. It's a Lisbon lemon, which I also learned from my faithful old gardening book. The Lisbon is the one with long fat thorns all over it.

Gingerly at first I trim the branches back with my not-so-faithful blunt secateurs. Unless I use the very tip of the tool, the blades tear at the stems rather than cutting clean, which is what I'm aiming for. The other thing that's not working too well is that the cuts should be above nodes and I'm not really sure that I'm getting that right. I find it difficult to tell the difference between a leaf bud and a node. I do the mental equivalent of closing my eyes and make the first cut. No hide, no Christmas cake, as my grandmother Foddy used to say.

The angle of the cut is important, I remember reading. It must be more or less at 45 degrees so water runs off the branch and not into the join. I manage, more or less.

I kick myself for not paying greater attention to Dad when he was pruning. All I can really remember him saying was to prune so the sun could reach every branch.

Gradually I pick up pace, beginning to enjoy the sparse, streamlined appearance of the tree although the thorns are ripping into me. Piles of cuttings accumulate at my feet and citrus scent fills the air. Bees hum around my hands. Are they angry? Snip, snip, snip.

I've started talking to myself.

'Take a bit more off this one. That's better. Now for this side. Hmmm … doesn't look the same length as … just another cut here …'

When I stand back to admire my handiwork I see the poor old lemon is half the tree it used to be. Perhaps I've gone too far and it will die. 'Where's the bloody book? Ouch!'

My battered old gardening book is half-buried under the cuttings and I've drawn blood yet again.

I mutter my way through the instructions … to revive old lemon tree blah blah … cut with a downward angle … bear on new growth … next season's crop …

Well, it sort of matches the illustration, although I might have gone a tad too far.

… most old lemon trees will improve with drastic cutting back …

It'll be all right then.

Pruning best done (oh no) in the spring. Bugger.

I have to catch up with Greg and work out an arrangement with him. We told Brian we would keep the tenant farmer thing going, but the details need to be sorted. Settlement on Grassy had taken three months, partly because the contract of sale was tangled up with the original lease agreement, apparently a standard format, between Brian and Greg. When our city solicitor asked to see us and we discovered its contents, we were just a little shaken.

Reading from the long document before him and watching for our reactions, the solicitor quoted: 'The owners agree to work in the plantation from time to time' (but we're not farmers!) '… provide all plant machinery' (like what?) … 'for a period of five years … ' (we could be dead by then!).

I recall that a hot flush crept across my scalp as the solicitor looked up from the document and said: 'I don't imagine that's what you have in mind.' Smile. 'Let's be clear about this. Do you want the farmer bloke to stay on?'

You bet, we told him, at least until we get the hang of things and decide whether we want to try farming the place ourselves or hire someone to do it.

'Then I would suggest you talk to the tenant farmer and come to a simple, straightforward agreement that suits both parties. Meanwhile, I will advise their solicitor that the contract of sale needs to go ahead separately from the lease agreement.'

No problem.

Meeting up with Greg is going to be easy, because he's usually here about four days a week, vanishing into the bananas and doing whatever it is he does. In fact, he turns up at the crack of dawn two days after Christo's gone to Sydney.

The noise of his arrival gets me out of bed in a hurry. I push my glasses onto my face and move to our bedroom window, which is right above the packing shed where he's parking his 'good' ute. I can't see him, but I hear him talking to his red kelpie, Dizzy, which means he'll soon be starting up the pared-down red farm ute he keeps here. Better get dressed.

After several attempts, the red ute cackles into life like a tree full of kookaburras with sore throats, Dizzy yelping deafening encouragement. The commotion sends Bindi into a tail-wagging frenzy and she keens in excitement.

Spluttering and rumbling to the top of the hill, gears crunching, the farm ute reaches our house with Dizzy leading the way and Bindi streaks off to run and tumble with her.

It's only 6.30 am, daylight saving time. Reluctantly I drag on jeans and a T-shirt and hobble to the veranda to wave Greg down.

'How ya goin'?' he asks, climbing down from the patched bucket seat. A floppy cloth hat is jammed onto his head, shorts and shirt stained black with sticky banana sap and heavy boots protecting his feet.

'Got some bananas for ya,' Greg calls out, giving me an easy smile. He's quite a good-looking young bloke with an open face, fit and strong from the hard manual labour and all that walking up and down hills; in his thirties I reckon. He strides to the back of the ute and hefts out a whole box full of just-ripening bananas with perfect, unmarked skins. They're arranged in a neat pattern, slotting into each other for perfect fit and presentation. There must be a hundred bananas there. How can I eat them all before they go off? Christo doesn't like bananas. Or mangoes.

'Thanks. Thanks a bunch.' I kick myself for the weak, inadvertent pun. It's because I'm nervous about having to talk to someone I hardly know about something I know very little about.

Dizzy and Bindi are rolling and jumping around each other in some weird dog dance. There are 8 hectares around us but, like children, they find the best place is right at your feet.

Dizzy waggles over to greet me with a playful leap, offering her head for a pat. 'She's gorgeous,' I tell Greg, which brings a jealous Bindi to my side. There's enough energy in those two wagging tails to stir a wallaby stew.

'Dizzy, in the truck,' Greg instructs, and she cocks her heads on one side to be sure he means it. 'Go on.'

Bindi follows, prancing around the ute.

I prepare myself to get down to business. 'Greg, our solicitor thinks we should have a new simplified contract ... you know, so we both know where we stand ... er, the rent and how we determine it.' I blather on. 'Don't worry, we're not going to change what you're already paying at the moment but the solicitor says it should be in writing and ... um, do you have insurance, stuff like that ... maybe something in there about the use of poison sprays ...'

I feel so awkward, but Greg just nods and waits for me to finish. 'Uh-huh. Yeah, a contract's fine with me.'

Surely he can see the relief on my face. 'Well, I'll get him to draw one up and show it to you. If there's anything in it you have a problem with, we'll just sort it out.' Some negotiator.

'No worries,' Greg replies, smiling. He turns to look over Grassy. 'You like it here? It's a top spot.'

'Yes, we do. We are so lucky.'

'What do you think you'll do with the place?'

'No idea at the moment. Too soon to say, really.' I don't think I'll tell him my wild dreams of turning the whole place into a fantastic garden for tourists, building a wedding chapel with an ocean backdrop, or showing movies in the greenhouse. He might not understand.

'We will probably rent the house out for a couple of years till we decide what to do.'

'That'd be a shame, now you've just bought it.'

We yarn on for a while, relaxing into the relationship, and I learn he's originally from Sydney where he was a metallurgist. But the area around here got under his skin and the farming bug bit. He's been doing the bananas at our place for five years. They're a good cash crop if you have a market, he tells me.

He's also bought some acreage up towards the highway, where he's started to farm avocados, several different varieties that will give him a year-round crop. He's planted bananas, too.

Greg is passionate about native plants and won't have exotics on his home acreage. 'Blue quandongs and lilly pillies mostly. The quandong's a really beautiful tree, gets these blue fruit on it in the summer. Birds love 'em. I've got some golden penda, too.'

I listen hard, trying to learn, but what's a quandong? What's a golden penda?

'You've got a golden penda in your garden, just there.' He points to a shrub near the mandarin tree and says it will be covered in yellow flowers any day now.

'You need to prune it back after it flowers to make it bush out. See how leggy it is.' Well, actually …

Behind Greg, on the horizon, I notice that the sky is low with angry gunmetal grey cloud and swatches of rain are falling into the sea. Struggling through the cloud mass, shafts of sunlight lay down two stripes of silver on the ocean, one just beyond Grassy and the other far out to sea.

Our conversation has lapsed. 'Greg, thanks again for the bananas. I'll get the solicitor to prepare a contract next week and we'll keep it simple. Just the rent agreement, annual reviews, how much notice we have to give each other, that sort of thing.'

'Yeah. No worries. Look, I'm probably going to be out of your hair in a year or two anyway now I've got my own place.'

'Oh. Uh-huh … Well, I'll give you a yell when the contract's done.' The ute rumbles to life, Dizzy sitting pertly in the passenger seat. 'See ya.'

And then the penny drops. Greg's planning to move on, build up his own farm, scale down here. What on earth are we going to do with 7.2 hectares of bananas?

chapter four

'Keep the layers level, because bacteria
work horizontally and the earthworms vertically.'

Compost tip from *Esther Deans' Gardening Book: Growing Without Digging*

My father Hector sold insurance for a living but all his life tilled the soil, any patch of it he could find, for pleasure. Born of poor Scottish parents, he was raised in the lush countryside of Cheshire in England and, as a boy, lived and worked on farms.

He emigrated to Australia, as an assisted farm labourer, in 1923 when he was eighteen and worked on dairy farms and market gardens in Victoria for three years before moving to New South Wales — just in time for the Great Depression.

He did a stint as an SP bookie, carted pumpkins, took odd jobs at fairs, worked as a labourer and did relief work; single men were allowed only one-and-a-half days of paid work a week.

For almost five years he, like many other able-bodied men, was unemployed and the experience gave him a lifelong passion for socialism and the trade union movement. Living in a tarpaper shack has a way of doing that to you.

Hec Chalmers was tall and well built, a handsome man who spoke with a lilting, modulated North English burr. No one would ever guess he had left school at the age of eleven — he was an easy conversationalist and very charming. Perhaps that explains how he started to move up in the world, becoming a life insurance salesman in 1935. He also started writing at about that time, quite an unexpected development in a man who had been the class dunce. But he'd always been an avid reader.

As World War II erupted, he and his mate Frank Cribbens wrote pamphlets about the perils of sexually transmitted diseases and sold them to young soldiers (for one and three pence). Then, at the age of thirty-six, he and Frank joined the AIF and sailed for Singapore … and almost four years incarceration in Changi.

After returning from the war weighing a bit over 57 kilograms, he married my mother Norma, twenty years younger and the daughter of friends who had also lived rough in bushland on Sydney's outskirts. I was born in 1947.

Dad always loved the idea of self-sufficiency and, in the first house he and Mum owned, at Wynnum, on Moreton Bay in Queensland, he dug up the backyard to produce an abundance of vegies year-round.

He also raised chooks (thanks to Mum's impulsiveness), harvesting the fresh eggs as well as killing a chicken when we needed one. I can still see him dunking the headless body in a bucket of hot water before stripping it of feathers.

Towards the end of his career with the Mutual Life & Citizens Insurance Company, he was a divisional manager and had paid off our second house and 2 hectares of volcanic farmland at Manly, where he became a serious weekend farmer growing, among other crops, bananas. Hmmm …

So with our tenant farmer's revelation that he'll be leaving on my mind, I ring Mum. 'Do you think Christo and I could farm the bananas ourselves?' I ask her, trying to recall whether Dad ever seemed to be stressed out trying to cope.

All my memories of that time are happy ones. Dad, tanned and panting a little from the humidity, sweat dripping off the end of his nose and a handkerchief, knotted at four corners, covering his head. The black snake Mum discovered in the pump shed, empty kerosene tins Dad filled with coal and lit every winter under the citrus trees to keep them free of frost, a paddock of pretty blue lupins that would be dug into the soil as green manure, strawberries poking up through holes in long rows of black plastic, the hiss of metres-high sprinkler jets as they spun and spurted, and the year we had so many bananas Mum had to invent a recipe for banana jam so they wouldn't be wasted.

'Well, dear,' Mum replies a little guardedly. 'Hec had only 3 acres.' That's only 1.2 hectares in today's measure.

'But could Christo and I manage, do you think? Dad just did it at the weekend.'

There's a moment's silence and I can picture her sitting there thinking about how she will find exactly the right words of support and, if absolutely necessary, of advice. Mum hates to discourage enthusiasm, her stock in trade.

'Bananas are a lot of work, dear. And, you know, your father never made a penny out of the farm.'

'Well, there are two of us. And this is a going concern.'

For Christo, I know the prospect of hard physical work would never be a deterrent. He's far from being a macho man, but he enjoys heavy work.

And I'm willing. Egging me on are the stories Dad told me of Louis Bromfield, a US journalist who revolutionised farming practices in the 1950s. In a time when the chemical fertilisers that produced fast crops were also turning farmland barren, Bromfield used super-phosphates only to grow green-manure crops that he ploughed back into the soil. He also let his pigs free-range to plump them up and housed chickens in the barn where their droppings combined with the hay to form rich compost.

His property, Malabar Farm, became an international showcase for organic farming methods. A journalist farmer with ethics, imagination and success, he was a bit of a hero to Dad, and to me. He was young when he went farming, though.

Mum is advising caution. 'You know, I would let things keep going the way they are for now. Greg isn't planning to leave right away, is he?

'No, thank goodness. It'll be a year or two.'

'Well, why don't you get the feel of things for a while. Christo has a job and you're getting some freelance work, plus there's a bit of income from the farmer. Just relax. Enjoy the adventure.'

It's now late May, and there's gloomy news from the local real estate agent who's been trying to find a tenant for Grassy Head. Although several people have looked at the house in the past few weeks, there are no takers at $240 a week, which, as the minimum we need to keep the mortgage at bay, is more than other people around here are charging.

I remember Janet saying Kempsey is the second poorest shire in New South Wales, with high unemployment. 'I'm afraid your house is almost too nice,' the agent says apologetically.

She tells me that she's very particular, and doesn't want a house-share, or people with dogs. 'Next thing you know they'll put an old caravan on the place and start growing marijuana.'

Heaven forbid!

And some people have been put off by the steep drive up from the packing shed to the house. 'Nonsense,' I respond, 'there's nothing wrong with the drive.'

Grudgingly, the agent agrees. 'I know. There's no pleasing some people. But I suppose it might be a bit tricky coming up that hill when it rains.'

I can't believe anyone would pass up the chance to live here and find myself getting quite cross. 'It's not as if they're buying the place!'

The agent has heard that the new people running the Stuarts Point Tavern are looking for a house to live in. Why not approach them?

So I invite them up for a look. They love the view, love the three bathrooms, love the bushland and don't mind about the bananas. It's everything they want, except … their teenage daughter has a pony and our property isn't fenced. Sorry.

Next?

'Maybe we should offer to fence it, just around the house,' I suggest to Christo at beer o'clock on the veranda. Now that the days are shorter, knock-off time is getting earlier and earlier.

'How are we going to do that? We're only up here every few weeks, we certainly can't do it ourselves and we're not here to organise someone to do it for us.' The voice of reason. 'Let alone the cost. And do we want a fence?'

It's starting to get chilly as the sun slips behind the national park, leaving the farmland and forest before us in shadow. The last of the light fans out over Grassy Head, blushing it with gold before disappearing entirely.

Time to go in. 'Would you like a fire tonight?'

'That would be lovely, darling.'

As I watch him confidently arrange a crosshatch pattern of twigs and set it alight, I remember our first camping holiday (well, my first, he'd been in the Scouts!) when it rained all the way from Wee Jasper on the Murrumbidgee to Lakes Entrance in south-east Victoria.

Even in the teeming rain, using a half-sodden toilet roll, he'd managed to create fire while I, safe inside our new, you-beaut tent, prepared enough lamb and barley stew for a crowd. (No, we didn't have a camping fridge.)

That would have been the summer of 1982, in a year when drought crippled so much of eastern Australia. We had found the only rainfall. A holiday never forgotten. Setting up camp in torrential rain, catching my first trout on the Goodradigbee River … and my second, unspectacular but heartbreaking, miscarriage.

The fire is crackling away as Christo returns from collecting an armload of wood from under the house, where the previous owner, Brian, thoughtfully left us a great pile of offcuts. We settle in with a heavy Rutherglen red to talk about things.

We think we can afford to keep both mortgages serviced if the agent doesn't find a tenant, as long as my freelance work doesn't dry up and Christo's job is secure, and there's no reason to suppose that either situation will change.

Selling Bondi Junction isn't really an option right now, with Alix still at home. Besides, we love our Sydney house, all blue and yellow, cute outside and streamlined inside, with a bedroom downstairs where Alix has the privacy a teen needs.

Into our second bottle of red, the picture is very rosy and the path is clear. I will have to spend every couple of weeks here to keep the grass cut and the house looked after, and by Christmas we'll have to have something sorted out.

'If we're going to more or less be living here, though,' says Christo seriously, 'we're going to need the right tools to keep the place in good order, including a tractor.'

A tractor? Aren't they dangerous? The thought horrifies me, recalling news stories about people being pinned under them for hours … even days. 'Can't we just hire someone who knows what they're doing?'

'Well, yes, maybe. But there are other tools we should have here. A generator for when the power goes. A chainsaw, probably. A decent brushcutter.'

'You mean a weed-trimmer thingo. We've got one.'

He raises a patient eyebrow. 'That thing was meant for suburban lawns, and it's electric.'

'We'll buy a long lead …'

'Honey, that'll do for a little while, but this place is big. How are you going to keep it under control when the weather warms up? The grass is already almost chest high.'

'But that's why I bought the mower. The man in the shop said it's just one model down from the model a professional mowing person uses. It'll whiz through this grass. You'll see.' He's such a worrier.

Winter falls into a pleasurable pace, especially for me because I am here at Grassy, discovering the newness of everything. The golden pendas have doused their fluffy blossoms now, their shimmering display all over in a few weeks.

Our lives slip into a pattern woven between Grassy and Bondi Junction. Christo and I drive up from Sydney, he stays the weekend and then he leaves me here for two or three weeks before coming back to collect me.

The trip is routine as we become familiar with the highway and its idiosyncrasies. There are patches where it's very slow because of roadworks, and on every journey we see progress towards making the Pacific Highway wider, straighter and safer. It can't happen too soon.

Twice on the southern run we are held up north of Buladelah behind several kilometres of stationary vehicles after accidents. On one of those occasions we take the dusty road west through Booral and Stroud, playing tag with dozens of other cars and trucks following a circuitous detour around this horror stretch of highway that has claimed so many lives.

From Bondi Junction it takes roughly six hours to get to Grassy, which neatly divides into two-hour revive-and-survive breaks and, after a bit of trial and error, we establish a regular itinerary.

Heatherbrae is two hours from Sydney, so we pull off the highway at the roundabout there. Although there's a Hungry Jack's and a KFC, we go for the local pie shop for a wee and a pie, generally in that order. If we're really hungry, the order is a pie with mushy peas and somehow we usually manage to arrive at mealtime (that is any time after 11 am).

Bindi enjoys the break too and comes to know the best sniffing spots in the semi-landscaped bush around the pie shop. She's been known to have a pie, too, no particular preference …

Normally I drive the second shift to the Taree turn-off, pulling off the road briefly there so Christo can take the wheel again. This is the home stretch, though we often stop in Kempsey to shop for groceries, and 30 minutes' later we turn off the highway onto Stuarts Point Road, keen to see all that's familiar and welcoming.

Very little has changed: the alpacas are sitting under the trees at the corner house, there's a 'No vacancy' sign swinging outside the Yarrahapinni B&B and the Peace & Paradise B&B farther along is booked out too.

The green slopes of the macadamia plantation at Three Figs, as always, look neat and freshly mown. Outside the dear little Uniting Church at the Barbers Lane junction, the three grevilleas are in golden bloom and, opposite, the whiteboard wired onto the fence announces the next monthly meeting of the Rural Fire Service.

The final landmark is the sign advertising handmade crab nets, fixed and collapsible, outside a house on the last hill before we get to Stuarts Point. Every time we drive by the sign I make a mental note; I must get one, and a tinnie with an outboard motor.

It's a little after 9 pm and Alix is on the phone. 'You can't be going to bed,' says the nineteen-year-old, who never calls it quits before 1 am, or midnight if she's tired. Just like her father.

'But I've had a big day,' I retort.

'Yeah, right. What's to do up there? Let's face it, Mum, you're bored because there's no TV.'

Just before she called I had settled down on the veranda in my $10.98 portable roll-up camp chair (with beer pocket), engrossed in the progress of a scattering of fishing boats, mast lights winking as they trawled for snook and snapper beyond Grassy.

'Even if I had telly, I wouldn't be watching it.'

'Mum, it's the country. There's nothing to do there. But you sound happy, so I'm glad.'

I could tell her about Greg's plans and that the two of us might have to become banana farmers to survive, but I'm in denial.

So I tell her instead about two magnificent birds I saw circling slowly above the national park, riding the thermal currents with massive wings outstretched and crying in piercing unison. They're ospreys, according to my borrowed book on birds, hawks that are fish-eaters.

'These ospreys, Alix, they build their nest 30 metres up in dead trees within 2 kilometres of water, and they mate for life. We might even have some nesting at our place.'

'That's interesting,' she replies without conviction. I suppose you had to be there, staring into the blue, eyes stinging, for the few brief minutes it took them to cross the sky.

Maybe it's a baby boomer thing.

'I'm very happy, darling, and I've had a wonderful day. Thanks for calling.'

'Night, Mum. Love you.'

Bacteria work in horizontal layers, earthworms vertical. Make sure your compost layers are level, warns Esther Deans, and that's why I'm reciting her mantra in my head.

While Christo is away I'm determined that this time, for the first time, my compost is going to come up to the right temperature (that's 180 degrees) with the help of good bacteria. When it cools, earthworms will colonise the pile and in a few months I'll have bucket loads of earth-fragrant, crumbly, potent material for my soon-to-be planted vegie garden.

Nature goes to no effort and still manages to produce worm-filled compost from fallen leaves. (Or is that humus and, if it is humus, how is it different from compost? Oh, well.)

Back in Sydney I tried to make compost but, after three years of unfailingly transferring vegie peelings from the kitchen sink down two flights of stairs to a black plastic composter in the courtyard, all I managed to produce was dried-out vegetable peelings. I don't want to talk about the leaking worm farm in the laundry.

This time I will persevere, following Esther Deans' instructions exactly. Her garden in the northern suburbs of Sydney, where flowers and vegetables and herbs grew in prolific success, was a showplace in the 1970s and '80s. And compost is the key to success.

According to Esther, compost must be made on soil, the most important factor because the bare earth brings with it magnetic rays, radiation and other useful forces to aid nature in its work. Well, I don't know about magnetic rays, but Esther certainly knew her onions. Photos in her book on no-dig gardening prove it.

Her recipe is to cover shrubby cuttings about 25 centimetres deep with well-tempered layers of leaves, lawn clippings and vegie scraps separated by fertiliser to get the bacteria going, some manure and lime or dolomite and, finally, a hefty layer of soil.

Sounds straightforward enough.

Esther's technique includes plenty of air so the rotting pile doesn't smell sour: good ventilation. The commercial bin I used had no vents or holes. Maybe that was the problem at Bondi Junction.

For a compost bin, I prise off the bottom panels of a metre-square timber packing crate but it's not easy with a mattock — my only option, really, since my other choices are a Swiss Army knife, a spade or a garden fork. It splits the timbers at the nail joins and the result is a bit rickety, but it'll do the job.

I find a spot for it between the shadehouse and the garage where it's out of sight, and set down a layer of twigs. On top, I tip the kitchen scraps from the small black plastic bucket that I salvaged from the worm farm disaster.

Peering into the bin, I'm a bit disappointed to see that four days' worth of vegie peelings, two eggshells and the skin of six bananas doesn't cover the layer of cuttings. I guess compost works faster if you have a family.

Next, fertiliser. But I don't have a car to go and buy some and the Point is 7 kilometres away. I know … the Clydesdales down the hill. With Bindi on her lead (she's never seen a horse and I'm not taking any chances), we set out down the gravel drive. Greg's not in the packing shed, but several bunches of green bananas hang heavily from ropes hooked onto a metal track overhead. Bindi sniffs at a well-chewed work boot lying outside on the gravel. Dizzy's, no doubt.

I still can't get over how many bananas there are on our property. They cover every square centimetre of the steep hill between the packing shed and the house, and line the road on both sides, some propped up with 3-metre long wooden stakes to support the bulging loads ripening under plastic bags.

At the bottom of the road we stop at the mango tree, noxious lantana reaching high up into it to show off its pretty pink, yellow and red flowers. Damn this stuff. Dad had to get rid of a lot of it at the Manly place, and Christo and I are going to have our work cut out for us too.

Looping Bindi's lead over a handy star picket, I tug at one of the long tendrils strangling the mango tree. I give it another good yank, scratching my hands and exposed arms on its spiny wood and releasing its spicy fragrance.

No one's around (apart from us, only our neighbour Mark and the bloke who feeds the horses use the road, I think) so I slip off my T-shirt to protect my hands and snap some of the long-reaching vines. It won't kill the lantana but at least the top portion will die off and then it's a matter of digging out the roots.

One thick piece refuses to break or release its hold, so I swing on it with all my weight, tumbling back onto the ground as it comes free. Now my torso is covered in scratches too, but it feels good to be out here doing something physical.

'That'll slow the bloody stuff down,' I tell Bindi.

Popping my T-shirt back on, I stand on tiptoes to try to see over the scrub to the dam. I'd like to go over there, but I'm not game. Even with the protection that Bindi's rampaging progress would provide, I am afraid of snakes.

As a general life philosophy, I totally agree with whoever said, 'The only regrets you have in life are the risks you don't take'. This particular risk, though, I can easily turn my back on.

The horses have heard us coming and amble to the fence along the property line, three wonderful Clydesdales and a couple of Shetlands. They're expecting food, not a dog.

On cue, Bindi barks her head off and they lumber away, disappointed, which gives me the chance to collect two plastic bags of sundried horse poo. Fantastic!

My first farming project is coming together. The hill back up to the house winds me, but I'm in heaven as I crumble the horse poo onto the food scraps, spade a layer of soil on top to make it all neat and then water the pile well. Smells great.

The grass around the house isn't anything like lawn. It's several different grasses, some quite wispy, some flat and broad-leaved, and there are plenty of cobbler's pegs. My friend Rosie reckons she never weeds as such; she just pulls them out as she walks past and that way it doesn't seem like a chore. Eventually you get all the weeds, she says. Mind you, Rosie lives in a townhouse with a shady courtyard garden.

I try that along the concrete path that runs the length of the back of the house, where the only things growing are cobbler's pegs and marigolds. I've never liked marigolds because of their acrid smell, but Greg tells me they repel nematodes, which attack the roots of plants. The marigolds will stay.

Rosie's technique seems to be working along the path and Christo swears we'll get rid of the cobbler's pegs if we keep mowing. But some of the grass is about 60 centimetres high, with seed heads, and it's very dense. This is Rhodes grass, imported from South Africa because it is terrific stock feed apparently, but a problem if it gets out of hand because it burns at very high temperatures.

The Rhodes grass is too tall for the mower, so I rig up the weed-trimmer and plug it into the extension cord. I've seen Christo use it, slashing in wide arcs to lay the grass at his feet, and as I get into the swing of it I find it much more efficient than mowing, although the stringy grass keeps clogging up the trimmer so I need to stop frequently to clear the jam. And there are rocks everywhere, shredding the line as it flinches against a sharp protrusion.

Swiping the tool from side to side, I plough on down the hill past the mango, cutting a wide, impressive swathe.

The undergrowth is getting denser and, as I approach an overgrown track that separates the home orchard from a stand of bananas, I check to see if I have enough cord to reach the end of this patch. I'm almost at the limit.

Swinging with all my energy, I sweep deeply into the grass. Nearly there. I slash hard to the right, pleased to see the grass falling before me. I break through to the track.

Suddenly I smell something. There's a "poof" sound, a wimpy kind of bang, and a spark where the handle meets the cord. Well, that's it. The trimmer is buggered.

Propping it up against the garage wall next to the wheelie bin, I walk over to check the compost and …

'Bindi-i-i-i … '

My compost bin lies on its side, eggshells, banana skins and half-rotted bits of lettuce strewn all over the place.

Bindi arrives, looks and, before I can say pointlessly, 'Did you do this?' she's off into the bush, her tail wrapped protectively around her bum.

Damn.

Much as I love the time I spend at Grassy, it's great being at home to see more of Alix, eat out at cheap ethnic restaurants (not much sushi takeaway at Grassy) with friends, walk to the shops where I can buy anything and everything I want, have Caralyn Taylor do my hair (after all, she's been my hairdresser for thirty years) … and, of course, be close to doctors. Aaah, the joys of being in our fifties.

Luckily for me I'm healthy. Not fit, but healthy. Good blood pressure, low cholesterol, clean lungs, strong heart.

Christo has copped the short straw, with high cholesterol and an inherited ischemic disorder, but he is fit. He runs every day.

Christo and I are cooking dinner at Bondi Junction one evening when Alix calls from downstairs. 'Mum, Bindi won't come inside. There's something wrong with her.'

Bindi doesn't know she's a dog. She's part of the family, an inside dog, so this is most strange. 'Be there in a minute.'

Bindi turns her happy face to me when I get to the back door. 'Come on, in you come.'

She takes a tentative, slow step towards me, all the time wagging her tail. 'Come on,' I say gently, trying to see what's happening in the fading light. As I watch closely, she raises one hind leg and places it gingerly on the ground, but it collapses when she tries to put her weight on it. The plucky dog takes two more steps but it's obvious she's in trouble. Then I see the problem — both her back legs are lifeless.

'Mum, she can't walk. What's wrong with her?' Alix rushes out to the dog, frantic, and strokes her curls.

'Christo! Quick!' I try to keep the panic out of my voice, but it's impossible. How could she be paralysed?

Christo has hefted Bindi into his arms and is holding her close. 'You drive,' he says, but I'm shaking too much.

'No, I'll nurse her in the car. You drive.' Alix and I share the back seat, cradling the dog in our arms.

We can't find a parking spot outside the vet's, which is right on the edge of the residential area where there's meter parking. So Christo double-parks while we haul the legless dog out of the car and half-drag her to the wide concrete stairs that she usually takes at a run; the vet to her means playmates, lots of attention and crunchy treats.

There's no way I can carry her, but somehow I bundle her back legs into my arms, holding her as kids do when playing wheelbarrows as she gamely tries to find the strength in her front legs to get her to the top.

The nurse rushes us into the examination room where she and the vet lift Bindi onto a stainless steel bench and begin examining her; typically, instead of showing signs of distress, Bindi is making contented moaning sounds as Alix pats her head. She even tries to lick Alix's hand.

'A tick in her ear,' pronounces the vet, 'a paralysis tick. Uh-oh. Here's another one between her toes.'

Skilfully she removes the ticks with tweezers and places them beside Bindi, who's turning her head to see what's happening. 'See how swollen this one is with her blood?' She squashes it, dark blood spurting out. 'They've found two ticks, love,' I tell Christo as he comes into the room.

'I'll keep looking,' the vet says, adjusting her glasses before combing carefully though Bindi's dense double coat. 'There might be more.' And there are. Two.

'I think you've got her in time, but it's too early to be sure. She looks like a strong healthy dog but four ticks can release a lot of poison. We'll have to see how she responds to the antidote, and even that puts pressure on the heart. She'll have to stay with us overnight.'

Why didn't we think of ticks?

Christo explains about Grassy and the vet nods. 'Bound to be plenty of ticks there.'

'What should we do to prevent her getting more ticks … if she recovers?'

'There are tablets, pour-ons and sprays you can use, but you also have to go over her every day during the tick season, which starts around August and goes through to midsummer. They're amazing things, ticks … one of the few parasites that actually kills its host. Except bandicoots. Ticks don't bother bandicoots at all. If there are bandicoots around, there are ticks.'

That night, our little house seems very empty without our inquisitive, incorrigible, infuriating dog.

'She'll be all right, won't she, Mum?' Alix asks.

And thankfully she is. She's weak but should be right as rain if we keep her quiet and cool for at least 48 hours.

We can do that. We will do that.

chapter five

'Something there is that doesn't love a wall,
That sends the frozen-ground-swell under it
And spills the upper boulders in the sun,
And makes gaps even two can pass abreast.'

'Mending Wall'
by Robert Frost

'Watch out for the wallabies.' Christo is on the phone to Alan. 'You'll probably see some grazing in the paddock on your right, but the silly buggers often look at you for a minute and then hop through the barbed wire right in front of the car. If you do see one hop across, watch for more. They're bound to be close behind.'

Alan and Kerrie are coming to stay for a week, driving up today from Sydney in their new Prado. Having talked us into buying a second-hand one, Alan convinced Kerrie it was the vehicle they needed so they could see more of the rough heart of Australia after he retires.

'Another thing,' Christo continues. 'When you come to the cattle grid, slow down. A water dragon hangs out just near there. He's usually pretty quick and disappears through the gaps, but sometimes he turns to stone in the middle of the track.'

Christo pauses, listening. 'No, don't bring any food. I'm making minestrone. Try to get here before dark if you can, so we can have a drink and watch the sun go down.'

Christo has the place looking wonderful. It takes about three hours to mow around the house, and that doesn't take in the home orchard, which has been a mess since my attempts to slash it led to the death of our line-trimmer. At least the weeds slow down during the cooler months.

But the 'big yard' is another matter. Littered with large rocks, furrowed and bumpy because of its previous life as a plantation of flowers, this is a sweaty, two-day job and one that I tend to put off when I'm writing. Fortunately Christo likes mowing, and he knocked it off at the weekend.

'Looks good out there now, don't you reckon?' He comes onto the veranda, plonks his favourite cowboy hat onto the green plastic 'dining' table we bought from the hardware store to make do, and flops down beside me on one of the matching ugly chairs. He sips a glass of ginger beer. I had every intention of making our own, remembering Mum nurturing a ginger beer bug when we were kids and what fun it was to feed it with sugar and watch it grow. But since coming here we've discovered a cordial from Buderim that makes a great ginger beer in an instant and, better still, no exploding bottles to create panic in the night.

'It looks great, darling.' Christo's red in the face, but it's from exertion not high blood pressure I reassure myself, and he seems as pleased as Punch with his day's work. Hot and sweaty … what a strange formula for happiness.

It's just on dusk when we hear the distant crunch of tyres on gravel, always an event here because it's so rare for a car to come up our drive.

'Must be the Bears,' Christo says, walking over to stand beside Bindi at the railing. She leans into him heavily and tilts her head for a pat.

Several seconds pass. Perhaps the sound we heard is not on our drive after all, and it's one of the neighbours who live up the 'main' road that ours branches off. But Bindi's pricked ears and twitching tail confirm that the car's definitely headed this way, even though we can't see it yet because the road dips out of sight for a couple of hundred metres or so and then is shielded by a solid curtain of bananas.

Suddenly we see it readying to take the sharp turn at the packing shed.

Christo ducks back inside to give his minestrone a quick stir. He's prepared it specially for these two very old friends, our first Sydney visitors. After all, this is an occasion, a housewarming of sorts.

With a bottle of sparkling wine to get us started, there's laughter and banter and plenty of drinking that night. They admire the view and listen to our plans over Christo's soup and crusty, fresh-baked supermarket bread. Their bitzer Pax, rescued from neglect by Kerrie and Alan several years ago and now living in comparative luxury, has curled up under the table near Alan's legs to discourage Bindi's playful interest. Pax is a sensible dog.

'So. Are you going to become banana farmers?' asks Kerrie. 'There certainly seem to be an awful lot of them. I don't think I'd like to tackle it.'

I explain that we have a new, simplified contract with Greg. 'The old agreement required the owners to work on the farm. Can you imagine us out there hacking away at those heavy bunches?'

Kerrie resists the urge to laugh. 'Maybe Christo … '

'Well, the contract we've signed with the young farmer is straightforward and sets out his needs and ours, with long periods of notice. But in a way he's already given us notice.'

'When's he going?'

'Well, it's a bit vague. Not that we mind. It gives us time to find our feet and work out what we're going to do here.'

The evening is getting cool, and Kerrie lets down her waist-length hair, shaking it free. She turns to Christo. 'Do you have any ideas?'

'Well, we're not ready to move here on a permanent basis yet, and I plan to keep working in Sydney indefinitely,' he responds.

Kerrie and I are into the second bottle of red now and gaining speed. Alan has switched his attention to a biography by Ion Idriess. 'And we have lots of plans,' I chip in. 'All sorts of things.'

'Gillian wants to become a marriage celebrant,' Christo announces. 'Have weddings down at the dam. She's obsessed by the dam near the mango tree, the one you drive past as you come onto our place. You can't see it from the road.'

It's true that I am fixated on the dam. I lie awake at night thinking about building a small landing out over the dam so brides can pluck water lilies for their bouquets as dazzling dragonflies skim over the water and frogs call from the banks. Gravel pathways will lead through regenerated native bush alive with bird song.

Alan snorts. 'Alive with mozzies, you mean.' Admittedly, we are all using tropical-strength insect repellent tonight.

Kerrie's all for the idea. 'You would be a wonderful marriage celebrant, I can see it now. And this is the perfect place.'

Not in Christo's opinion. 'It's a terrific dream, love, but we'd have to get council approval, put in toilets, have insurance, get the neighbours to agree to traffic on the drive. All sorts of stuff. And it would cost a fortune … '

'I know that, but … ' Why does he have to be so bloody practical? 'It would be good to have some return from this place after Greg goes, and I love the idea of sharing it with other people. It's just an idea … '

Kerrie won't be put off. 'It's a good idea, too. I think you could make it work. Can you take us down for a look?'

'No point, really, it's overgrown and there are probably heaps of snakes. But we will clear it one day.'

Emboldened by wine and Kerrie's enthusiasm, I reveal that I would also like to conduct funeral services. 'Not at the dam, though.'

Christo hasn't heard this particular suggestion before. He and Alan exchange eye-rolling glances. 'What do you think, Kezza?'

'I think you would be good at that, too. Have you done anything about it?'

I have, but the whole thing seems pretty complicated. There's a limit on numbers, and new celebrants are appointed only if there is community need, and I can't see me, a stranger, getting residents at Stuarts Point to sign a petition asking for my services. Still, I've compiled a list of celebrants from Kempsey to Nambucca and there's no one really local, so I'm hoping they could squeeze in one more.

'Speaking of weddings,' Kerrie says, 'what are you doing this year for your anniversary?' They were married on the same day as we were, 28 November, but five years' earlier.

'We haven't talked about it yet. We usually go out to dinner with Alix.' When there are only three in the family, it's all for one …

'But obviously that won't happen if we're up here. I've been thinking about it though, and I've already decided what we should do about presents.'

This gets Christo's attention. 'Have you now? Did you plan on telling me about it?'

I give him my best teasing grin. 'Yep. I don't know how I ever thought we could manage here without the right tools.' A mock worried look from Christo. 'I reckon for our anniversary, we should buy ourselves a top-of-the-line brushcutter.'

'You heard her,' Christo exclaims. 'At last she's starting to realise that we need the proper equipment. I want a chainie, too.'

'Boys' toys,' Kerrie mocks.

Alan slaps his book shut and stands. 'Don't you women have any respect?'

And as Pax and Bindi test out each other's sleeping arrangements for the night, Pax deciding on Bindi's creaky trampoline and Bindi opting for Pax's lumpy purple pillow in some unfathomable canine trade-off, we call it quits and head for bed.

Next morning, while Kerrie and Alan are following the tourist trails with a collection of maps and brochures I've been compiling for visitors, we get to work weeding the home orchard. Or Christo does. He's cut down what he can without wrecking the super-mower on hidden rocks, and begins to tackle the large weeds with the mattock.

He's working over near the nectarine tree. I'm raking up all the long grass felled by the line-trimmer, because I have a plan. I've read of a quick composting method in a book I borrowed from the Point library: you make a pile of grass clippings a metre high, wide and deep, mix it with plenty of organic fertiliser and water it. Then, if you turn it every day, it will rot down in a few short weeks.

My arms tingle pleasantly as I begin to form the grass into a pile using an old hay fork Christo discovered in a patch of cow cane somewhere; it's the real thing.

When the pile is about 30 centimetres high, I sprinkle it lavishly with blood and bone. The smell doesn't bother me. In fact, I quite like it. Bindi likes the taste.

The pump bringing water from Mark's dam thrums away as I drench the top of the pile. Quietly confident, I heap more grass onto the first layer. It isn't coming together as well as I'd like, though, the grass refusing to be arranged in an exact square. I wonder how to make the sides as deep as the middle; so far, it's more like a small haystack than the cube described in the book. Maybe the shape isn't really important — the depth is probably the critical thing, but it's getting wider as I go, too.

Walking around the pile, I try to push the heap into a square but the sodden mass resists me as if it's a stone wall. However, I refuse to obsess about the shape. I will pile all the grass as best I can and finish the job. It is not meant to be an architectural marvel or a demonstration for television viewers and I have employed the theory perfectly.

Stopping for a breather, I peer under the mango tree and through the bare branches of the nectarine tree to see Christo lifting the mattock high above his tanned bare torso.

Back to my compost, I reach higher and higher to place forkloads of grass on the swelling organic stack in trance-like rhythm. Heave the grass, scatter the fertiliser, water well; heave the grass, scatter the fertiliser, water well; heave the grass, scatter the fert …

The flow from the hose by my side dribbles to a stop. 'Christo, what have you done to my water? Is the hose kinked?'

It's a touch worse than that. 'I've wrecked the watering system,' he yells back 'That's what.'

Uh-oh. I walk over to where he's standing near the pump, leaning on the mattock and looking very angry.

His hands are all muddy and there's dirt smeared on one cheek.

'An irrigation pipe. Didn't know it was there.' He points with the mattock, waggling it dangerously around Bindi's eager head.

'And you cut through it?' He nods, grimacing.

'With the mattock?' Another grimace.

Hence no water. 'And now, there's a bloody flood out here, so I've had to turn the pump off.'

Thank God it wasn't the house pump. 'What are we going to do?'

'How the hell would I know? I don't even know if I can repair the pipe, let alone start the pump again. I don't know a thing about pumps.'

Perhaps I should have a look at it for moral support? But I see instantly that moral support won't solve this one. The plastic piping, engineered to withstand many extremes of nature, was never intended to deflect a mattock's blow. It's been chopped right through, just one precisely aimed cut, and the ground around it is like a swamp.

'The Point hardware store might sell things to join up plastic tubing. I'll go if you like.'

'No, I buggered it up. I'll go.' Sometimes when people are angry, it's better to leave things alone — but I can't help myself.

'You can't go like that. You should see your face,' I splutter. 'You look like a four-year-old who's been making mud pies.' Christo starts to laugh with me, shaking his head. What a crazy couple of incompetents.

We're having a quiet night, no television, Kerrie and I sharing a bottle of red on the veranda. Alan has switched from Idriess to a Gore Vidal novel while Kerrie is demolishing a cryptic crossword. Christo is reading too, and I'm just sitting and dreaming as usual when the subject turns to sausages. In particular, the famous sausages of Macksville.

The town has two locally famous butcheries, one right on the Pacific Highway that makes brilliant bratwurst and, a block away, Dangerous Dan's, purveyor of a range of gourmet sausages — lamb, beef, chicken, pork and kangaroo-flavoured with macadamias, Warrigal greens, honey and other things. Both butchers are award-winners, and Dan, the current mid-north coast champion, even takes his sausages to North Sydney markets once a month.

This night we've been eating an assortment of Dan's jumbuck and bushman snags when for some reason Christo makes a remark about frankfurts. But he can't seem to get his tongue around the word and instead of saying 'frankfurts' makes an unintelligible sound. We all laugh, Christo included, and he tries again, stammering.

'What's the word I'm trying to say?' he asks slowly, slurring his words slightly. We laugh a little, feed him the word, but I'm worried. Although he sounds drunk, he hasn't had a drink tonight. Christo retires and a few minutes later I follow him to the bedroom. 'Are you okay, darling?'

'T-t-tired,' he stammers, then says something else I cannot understand. It's pure gibberish this time and I can't make it out. I am aware of my heartbeat, strong and slow and pounding.

Once, long ago, I was a nurse. An image comes to mind of a patient blurting out a string of meaningless syllables as her brain was tossed about by a massive stroke. On her face, total confusion.

I try to blink the memory away as Christo gets up and walks around, obviously fighting some obstruction I can't see or feel so he can form the words in his head.

'My ... my ... '

Oh, God ... What's wrong with him? ... Why can't he speak properly? Is he having a stroke? ... Oh no, I'm going to throw up ... No, I can't ... I have to be calm ... Tell him it's going to be all right ... But ...

How can I ask him if he's having a stroke without saying the word? It'll terrify us both. Desperately I force myself to focus on how to ask him if he's having a stroke ... without actually using the word. 'Darling, would you like me to take you to Macksville Hospital?'

He shakes his head, and enunciates with excruciating effort, 'I think ... I am ... '

Fleetingly I think that his utterance would be funny in different circumstances. And I remember his previous stroke: the sweating and nausea, the staggering, the fear, the misdiagnosis in the emergency department ('a panic attack; take this valium and lie down until you feel better'), the tears and finally the relief in the hands of his specialist who made it right.

Christo paces restlessly around the bedroom, frustrated and angry, then pauses, concentrating to articulate a word that won't come.

'My, my, miger ... '

I smile with false calm, but I'm calculating that it will take me twenty minutes to drive to Macksville ... If I can drive ...

Or maybe Alan could … Pills. I should give him some tablets … Aspro? … Or a brandy … What?

'Migraine,' he spits out. 'A migraine.'

'You've got a migraine?' Shock. Disbelief. Is he in denial?

Christo suffers occasionally from neurological migraines that cause visual disturbances and numb his fingers, but a migraine that affects speech this way? That's never happened before.

'I think … I should … take … my … my … graine tablets.'

Christo climbs into bed as I bring him two pills, relieved to an extent that I can do something practical. But are the migraine tablets the right thing to give him?

I fake a bright smile and ask, as casually as I can, 'How about we leave for Sydney right now. I'll drive and you can rest. I'm wide awake.'

Liar.

His eyes are drooping, his breathing deep and slow. 'If I can just sleep …' I can't think what else to do, so I lie with him in the dark, circling his body with my arm and not daring to sleep.

Dawn comes gently across the ocean, a pale blue sky tinged with pink and a row of cumulus clouds clinging to the horizon. We've made it through to daylight, so I let myself fade into a light sleep until I hear our guests start moving about in the kitchen.

Over breakfast, I confide in Kerrie and Alan that I think Christo has had a stroke and they hug me warmly, squeezing tears from my eyes, and then out of the blue Christo's joined us — bright-eyed and bushy-tailed. I wish I could say I feel the same. I am an absolute wreck.

Still, the day does improve. Just before lunchtime Alan spots two humpback whales on the southern side of Grassy Head, powering north at breathtaking speed. We can see them clearly from the veranda, sometimes breaching in a spectacular splash of silver, sometimes slapping the surface of the churning white-capped sea with their muscular flukes.

As the two glorious giants leap and twist and toss in some primeval purpose we intrinsically treasure but will never fully comprehend, the enchantment overwhelms us. Misty eyes say it all. The annual winter migration of whales from the Antarctic has begun and we have a front-row seat.

After Christo chucked in his Education Department job in 1980 in Brisbane, where he was making programs for kids living in isolated parts of Queensland, to be with me, we lived in Sydney for quite a while. Then it was Brisbane, Auckland, Melbourne and back to Sydney. In total, thirteen homes in twenty-five years. We've made a huge contribution to several government stamp duty coffers.

In our various homes, we've made friends, often good friends, with our neighbours. (Although in the city once there was the elderly man with eight cats that materialised in a mewling mass from every dark corner when he set out a platter of slippery, bloody liver for them on the kitchen table where he was serving me coffee. He wasn't too flash.)

Getting on with your neighbours makes life easier, but you have to be one too, an attitude I probably owe to being raised on *The Water-Babies*, starring Mrs Doasyouwouldbedoneby.

Meeting the neighbours around here isn't as easy as sticking your head over the fence or turning up with a plate of freshly baked scones. We've chatted with Mark next door a few times about the weather, slashing and our informal arrangement about using water from his dam. He seems cool.

We haven't met any of the neighbours on the 'main' road yet, our contact limited to fleeting acknowledgement, a smile and a wave as we pass each other in billows of dust or slow to check for oncoming traffic at the T-intersection where the wheelie bins are left for weekly collection.

Much of this area used to grow bananas. Now it's native forestry timbers, cut flowers, peaches, macadamias, avocados, mangoes and untended properties where wattles battle it out with lantana and groundsel. Ours is the last of the banana farms.

From our place, only two houses are visible; forest and hills obscure the rest. Properties around Grassy are zoned for agriculture and tourism and can't be subdivided into blocks of less than 20 hectares. Hopefully that's how things will stay. Development is an evil word around here, and rightly so.

Getting to know neighbours Margaret and Jim was probably one of the best things that happened to us in the first few months of moving to Grassy, and it came about as a result of our ignorance combined, I suppose, with a genuine readiness to learn. Although we had never met, Jim phoned one evening and asked if he and his wife Margaret could come onto our property to remove an invasive weed that was growing near our shared boundary. Naturally enough, we said yes. Although we didn't meet them on that occasion, we came face to face with Jim a few weeks later.

As a rule, the only people who come right up the private road are Greg or Mark and his family and friends. If people turn towards our place, it usually means they're either lost or looking for Mark. Occasionally it's the unwelcome strangers who turn up in pairs to canvass our redemption with Bibles and fixed, sugary smiles.

One weekend, an unknown ute makes the journey up our hill and parks confidently outside the house, ejecting a tall, slim man of distinguished age and appearance, dressed in neat, grey overalls and gumboots.

'James,' he says to Christo, who's come out to see who the visitor is. 'From over the hill. Just wanted to introduce myself and swap phone numbers with you.

'Good to meet you, Jim,' Christo says. 'Would you like to come up on the veranda.' Jim follows him upstairs. 'Coffee?'

Jim fishes a small piece of paper out of his top pocket and hands it to Christo. 'No, thank you anyway. Here's our number.'

We've heard quite a bit about these two. They've lived here for well over twenty years and are known for their conservation activities. Jim and Margaret retired here after searching for paradise on the east coast for two years. At Grassy they found that their love of nature was matched by many of the locals who had recently won their campaign to stop sand mining at Middle Head. Grassy was also earmarked for mining, for the beaches here are rich in rutile.

Margaret and Jim were also involved in the move to have Yarrahapinni State Forest — our backyard — declared a national park, so Christo and I have a lot to be grateful for, and we are.

Jim hasn't seen his plantation of eucalypts from this perspective before, and his grey eyes squint in concentration as he examines the forest. On cue, two huge king parrots screech out of the gums towards us and whip around the house at eye level in all their red-and-green glory.

'My, the trees do look good, don't they?'

He and Margaret planted flooded gum and Sydney blue gum across from us just nine years ago, he explains, to replace bananas and control erosion on a steep site that is a mirror image of ours. The trees, excellent cabinet timbers, should earn them an income after another ten years or so.

My eyes are drawn to one particularly magnificent tree in the rainforest patch next to the gums. 'What's that one, Jim?'

It reaches high into the sky, its feathery lateral branches covered in clusters of brilliant green leaves.

'That one? That's *Elaeocarpus grandis*, the blue quandong.'

So that's the one Greg's so mad about. I can see why.

A few weeks later, Jim calls to invite us to tour their place and have morning tea with him and Margaret next time Christo and I are both here. 'Meet you at the mango tree at nine,' he says, and we're there with bells on.

Margaret and Jim have changed the face of their property. They farmed the existing bananas for a while, tried to get a macadamia crop going, experimented with avocados but, in the end, removed the irrigation lines and set about arresting the erosion.

With little experience to go on, they planted what they thought would work for the environment and themselves. On our tour of their property, twice the size of ours, we climb wide graded pathways past groves of rainforest and palms, tall trees and flourishing understorey. We tread respectfully through remnants of old-growth rainforest Jim and Margaret have cherished as sanctuary for fauna and flora.

As we stroll gradually uphill, Jim's eyes are constantly raking over the plant life, stooping to pull out the pretty yellow flowers of fireweed and stash the harmful plants in his overalls pocket for disposal later, or cursing at an escaped tendril of milk vine sneaking up the trunk of a planted ironbark.

Most trees are identified with the year of planting; each section has its own history of how and why and just who had a hand in its selection, for their obsession spawned a family tree of its own — daughter Wendy and her husband Chris, along with sons Michael and David, have become tenants in common of this enterprise and still help guide the forest's birth and growth. Another son, Greg, is a national parks ranger.

It takes more than an hour to climb the hill and dip down and up again to their cosy mudbrick house in a broad clearing and by then I have totally lost my bearings. We approach the house through an extensive vegie garden, alive with beans and cabbages and spinach and vines dripping with passionfruit.

Outside, a table is set up for morning tea and we meet Margaret at last as she brings homemade biscuits and offers tea, which is very welcome after our long walk.

Margie, Jim calls her. We sit in the shade and look around at cleared paddocks where a handful of cattle chew at the pasture. A dainty little bird with twitching tail feathers and a luminous blue breast joins us, pecking at the ground for crumbs we haven't yet spilled.

A superb wren, Jim says it's called. Of course. What else?

As we sip tea and munch homemade biscuits, we begin our relationship with these two interesting people: Jim intense and informative, Margaret petite and watchful like the wren. It's only when she gets up to clear the table that I notice her small feet are planted firmly in a pair of sturdy boots. I think I sense a friendship coming on.

chapter six

'You have to make time for cooking.
It's part of sitting around the table with
your family. It's part of the social process.
I mean, you'll destroy the fabric of
society if everybody goes around
munching a burger by themselves in the
corner and throwing away the container.
Pretty miserable, don't you think?'

Mildura chef and slow food advocate Stefano de Pieri

Spring is full of surprises. Scattered around the house, in all sorts of odd places, pockets of freesias have broken through the heavy soil to fill the air with sweet fragrance, and there's a patch of lemon thyme I've never noticed, flecked with pretty mauve flowers, growing beneath the African tulip tree.

The lemon, orange and mandarin trees are still bearing but they're also starting to produce intensely aromatic white flowers in preparation for next winter's crop. The peach and nectarine trees are showered in pink and white blossom.

Feathery yellow balls dot the self-sown acacia, the Sally wattles that are so common here, delighting swarms of native bees. A big green frog has come to stay, hiding down in the cool depths of a terracotta pot on the veranda.

Even my first no-dig vegie garden springs a surprise — a bush of cherry tomatoes I didn't plant has popped up unbidden through the layers of compost (store-bought in the end), lucerne hay and straw. The chilli bush is covered in green chillis about to turn red, there's enough sage to stuff a whole pig and, best of all, peppery rocket is growing in delicious profusion.

But there's a bad surprise as well. Caterpillars are eating the leaves of my cabbages and Brussels sprouts.

What to do? I shoot off an email to Ian in Melbourne.

His reply is swift and to the point. 'There's only one thing to be done about cabbage white butterflies: kill them!'

Cringing at the thought, I type back, 'That seems a bit radical. Isn't there some organic way to split the spoils with the cabbage white butterfly larvae? You know I hate killing things.'

Pragmatist that he is, Ian spells it out. 'It's the cabbages or the caterpillars. Your choice. The product I use is the go. Organic. It won't harm the beneficial insects, bees or mammals. And don't be too fussy about killing things; just think about roast lamb.'

As an aside, I boast that the rocket is doing so well it's strangling the cobbler's pegs.

No comfort from him on this one. 'Of course it grows well. What did you expect? It's a weed. Don't eat it myself.'

I ask for the product at the nursery in Macksville. 'This one will get rid of the caterpillars,' the woman there tells me, unlocking a glass-fronted cabinet. 'It's a very effective biological control, a bacterial stomach poison. The caterpillar ingests it and dies a few days later.'

'Oh dear,' I say meekly. The treatment sounds gruesome.

'Look, you could just pick them off,' she says, sensing my hesitation, and assures me it's what she prefers to do. 'Every morning, check the leaves and, if you find any caterpillars, remove them and put them somewhere else.'

This seems to be an ideal solution, and if she can do it …

It's amazing how many eggs a cabbage white butterfly can lay, dozens of tiny bright yellow balls sticking like glue to the undersides of all the leaves. To remove them I rub the leaves between my thumb and forefingers. The squishy feeling is extremely unpleasant so I try working with gloves and, after half an hour, have wiped off all the eggs and transferred all the caterpillars to blades of grass a few metres away.

My back and legs are aching with the unaccustomed bending, but I'm happy to have found an ecologically responsible solution that's also kind.

Incredibly, the next morning it's almost the same as it was: myriads of yellow eggs, plenty of fat caterpillars. The only difference is that there are even more holes in the leaves — I must have missed a few yesterday.

The next surprising thing I learn about the caterpillars is how perfectly they adapt their colour to blend in with the background, whether it's on the broccoli leaves or the cabbages. The way they match different plants is quite extraordinary.

What's more, the smallest caterpillars are able to squeeze in between the just-forming leaves that are still wrapped tightly together and the only way to get at them is to peel back the layers, ruining the vegies.

There is so much to learn when you move from an inner-city terrace to a farm in the country. The trouble is, by the time you've realised that picking caterpillars off sprouts, cabbages, caulis, broccoli and such doesn't actually work, you've lost the battle of the species and have to drive into Macksville to buy your vegies.

At least there's rocket for our sandwiches … bunches and bunches of it.

Macksville is our nearest real town, with pubs, banks, a council building, two supermarkets, three service stations and three thousand people. Therefore it's where we go when we have real needs: to do our washing, for instance. We don't have a washing machine at Grassy yet.

It's also very picturesque. Even the coin-operated laundry has a prime position on River Street, directly across the road from the Nambucca River and two doors from the old Star Hotel.

On our first visit to the laundry we discover that a load of washing takes about forty minutes, giving us exactly the right amount of time to enjoy a lazy round of schooners on the veranda while watching highway traffic trundle over the narrow two-lane bridge.

Macksville is just a dot on the map for truckies and tourists travelling the Pacific Highway, but it slows everyone down one way or another; two sets of lights in town interrupt their 100-kilometre-per-hour progress, bringing giant transports and cars burdened with surfboards and pushbikes to a standstill and causing traffic jams, especially in school holiday periods.

Though the Nambucca River was once the main transport system for bringing valuable cedar logs down from the hinterland, it is better known for its plump oysters and houseboats now all the cedar has been logged.

Sitting outside taking in the view of the slow-moving river and the incessant traffic is so mesmerisingly pleasant we stroll inside to order lunch from the bistro, named McNally's after the pub's first licensee way back in 1885.

Inside, old Tooth's Beer ads featuring sporting heroes hang on the walls (after all, this town is the home of New South Wales's oldest foot race, the Macksville Gift); grainy black-and-white photos tell the history of the industries that established Macksville — dairying, cedar-getting and grazing. They still raise beef cattle around here but the other rural pursuits have largely succumbed, economic rationalisation is killing off the dairy farms, ignorance and lack of foresight have ravaged the forests.

Christo ponders the menu. 'I'm going for the beer-battered fish,' he says, 'although I'm tempted by the burger.' The burger's my choice.

You couldn't eat better in a Sydney pub for the price, service, freshness and flavour. No waterlogged tomatoes in these side salads. No wilted lettuce. It's mostly local produce, and that includes the fish and beef.

'How about I go and get the laundry and we have a second beer?' Christo suggests, so we linger another half-hour before heading back down the highway for Grassy.

'Honey, I have a favour to ask you.'

He's concentrating on driving. 'Yep. Sure.'

'When we get back to Sydney, can I come to the neurologist with you? I would like to hear what he has to say.'

'I don't see why not. He's only going to tell me what I know already, that I had a migraine.'

How can he be so flippant? I want to talk to the neurologist myself and explain what I saw, how frightening it was. Ever since the night when Christo couldn't speak properly, I've been thinking back to what I call 'the night of the fish'.

We were living in New Zealand at the time and had just finished a dinner of grilled snapper and mash and moved into the lounge room to watch TV. Christo turned and said to me: 'Honey, I feel a bit weird. My left arm is numb and … my tongue feels, er, thick.'

In another life, I must have taken acting classes because what I saw then almost stopped my heart and I knew I had to hide my panic. The left side of Christo's face — all of it — had sagged into rubbery folds. I could see alarm in his eyes, but I smiled.

'Well, that's no good.' I got up and poured him a brandy. 'Here. Sip this slowly.'

I turned my eyes to the television while I gathered my thoughts and calmed my breathing, sneaking an occasional peek Christo's way.

Within a few minutes, however, the feeling came back to his arm and he relaxed. I didn't. 'I think there was something wrong with the fish,' he said. 'Sigatura poisoning, maybe. Anyway, I'm all right now.'

Maybe he was all right, but there was no way I was going to accept that he'd simply had a mild brush with a rare tropical fish poison. I went to the kitchen to phone the medical centre, describing the symptoms in a hushed voice as Christo watched television.

'How is he now?' the nurse inquired.

'Well, the feeling has come back and he says he's okay now … '

'Bring him to the medical centre tonight if you're worried. He might have had a stroke.'

But we didn't go. Christo insisted he was fine, that it was 'only' a migraine.

Well, he was right about the migraine … but he was wrong about it being 'only' a migraine. When he finally agreed to my pleas for a neurological consultation, tests revealed Christo had inherited a rare and only recently identified condition known as CADASIL (cerebral autosomal dominant arteriopathy with subcortical infarcts and leukoencephalopathy), a disorder that causes miniscule strokes in the capillaries of the brain, a disorder that had eroded the faculties of his much older brother over a period of fifteen years. The cure? There is none. Prognosis? Variable. Could he be a carrier? A fifty per cent chance. Treatment? Aspirin, daily aerobic exercise, no hard liquor, low-cholesterol diet, pills to ensure low blood pressure. And no stress.

Was this latest incident at Grassy only a migraine too? It couldn't have been. It was so terrifying. I am sure Christo has suffered another stroke, maybe not one as bad as the one in 2002, but a stroke nevertheless. Christo needs to face facts.

So I say my piece to the neurologist, describing Christo's speech loss in uncomfortable graphic detail. I feel awkward, as if I'm telling tales, but the doctor nods in understanding. He puts Christo through some basic tests — gripping his hands, walking a straight line and testing his knee-jerk reactions with a little hammer.

Is that all there is to it?

The neurologist returns to his desk, interlocks his fingers on the oak desk. Smiles.

'You seem in good shape. Still a little weakness on the right side. As for the incident with your speech, Mr Nicholson, it was a migrainous event.'

We've been married twenty-three years this month. According to Christo, who counts from the year he came to live in Sydney with me, it's twenty-four years. Either way, we celebrate on the anniversary of our wedding day.

'Only two days to go,' I remind him. We've come up to Grassy for a couple of weeks.

He looks a bit crestfallen. 'I know, I can't think of what to get you. Damn it. I should have bought something in Sydney.' We're both used to the convenience of last-minute shopping in the city, and our options up here are to go to Kempsey, half an hour away by car, where there's an enormous BIG W, or travel to the more sophisticated retail centres of Coffs Harbour and Port Macquarie, an hour's drive in opposite directions.

'I thought we'd settled on a brushcutter for our anniversary?' I know that it's his heart's desire and it's fast becoming mine.

'It's not a very romantic present.'

'I know, but we need it. We'll go out for a romantic dinner.'

His spirits lift. 'Really? You don't mind such a practical present?'

I don't mind at all. I'm lucky to have a husband who's funny and clever and loving. Not to mention patient: after cutting through the irrigation line, getting the pump started again was a triumph of perseverance over total ignorance, as he spliced together advice from Greg, the troubleshooting tips in the manual Brian had left for us and his own commonsense.

No, I'm actually quite excited about the brushcutter. Together we go into Macksville and test-drive a couple for weight and ease of use. Christo says the final choice is up to me. Hefting the second-biggest tool, the one with the $650 price tag, I swing it in a wide arc and back again to test my strength. The truth is it's a bit heavy for me but it has a shoulder strap that will take some of the burden. 'This is the one.'

We return home with our pride and joy to get ready for our big night at the Rocks. Christo shaves, I put on my face. We want to get there early for a look around. South West Rocks has changed quite a bit. Inevitably, its laid-back ambience and simple beauty have brought growth. Real estate prices have rocketed, the informal, knock-about country club building has been vacated for a flash new architectural statement, the ruins of historic Trial Bay Gaol now houses a museum and concerts are held there, the lighthouse-keeper's accommodation has become an upmarket B&B.

Unfortunately, the popularity of the Rocks has also spawned a garish shopping centre and developer-driven suburban sprawl we have to drive past to get to the beach. It's a shocker, and I shudder at the thought that mindless subdivision might one day overwhelm Grassy and Stuarts Point.

But there's one gem that withstands the onslaught of development, a slow food restaurant down near the beach where we've eaten once before: Geppy's. The place is run by chef Geppy Dezani, exponent of a cooking style that's all about seasonal local produce and culinary tradition. It's an Italian thing, the antithesis of fast food and bland flavour.

Geppy is behind the counter when we arrive, togged out in white jacket and black-and-white checked chef's trousers. His partner Catherine welcomes us as if we're old friends and finds us a table with a beach view.

'Happy anniversary, darling.' Christo toasts me across the candlelit table with a beer; I'm having Campari and soda.

'To us,' I reply dreamily. 'To slowing down, to not rushing through life.'

Our slow food is served at a congenial pace. Christo has the native Warrigal greens with parmesan and venison (which, the menu notes, is from fallow deer bred in a stress-free environment) in a berry sauce. I work my way through an antipasto plate of salami and tasty nibbles and then indulge in chicken cooked in creamy marsala sauce. We even have pud: tiramisu and panna cotta.

What a lovely anniversary. Slow is good.

I'm learning all the time; turning a cubic metre of sodden Rhodes grass with a fork is not possible. For me, anyway. My hayfork embeds itself in the heap and my back and arms can't take the strain of lifting it; a couple of tries convince me this is not going to work.

Bugger the instructions and the impossible 1-metre cube. I will spread the pile over three or four shallow, manageable metres of mulch below the peach tree to cover the existing terrace of rocks. This will transform the sharp step into a gentle slope, breaking down into nutrient-rich fodder for both the peach tree and the two lychee trees below it.

I'm sweaty but pleased with my solution. 'What do you reckon, Christo?'

'Seems to me it might be a very slow way to turn a terrace into a slope. Won't it take quite a long time to break down?'

'Nah. You'll see.'

After considering his specialist's advice, Christo says he wants to quit work. It's a good idea, I tell him. It will ease his stress, life will be calmer and he won't have to force himself out of bed early every morning to go running to beat the CADASIL.

We talk it through while we're at Grassy, where the air we breathe clears our heads and the sights and sounds separate us from worry. Four sleek brown birds with long tail feathers are gorging themselves on the tiny green berries of a nondescript small tree that grows in the shade of the awesome African tulip tree. Brown cuckoo doves, we've been told. The twisted branches sag under their weight as they twist and turn, sometimes hanging upside down, to reach the best berries.

'How will we manage with both of us out of work?' Christo asks, still unsure he's making the right decision. 'I'm not likely to get another job at my age.'

'Well, no, but for a start we can rent out Bondi Junction,' I say easily. Alix has decided to move into a flat with her friend Hayley. 'We'll get a good return for it and we can live very cheaply here. Maybe you could re-train, get a job in Macksville or Kempsey, something that interests you. Become a barman, a barista. You look great in a bow tie.' This makes him smile, but I mean it.

The plan is straightforward enough, but when Christo returns to work and resigns his boss asks him to stay on in a permanent part-time role. Now it's getting complicated.

Kerrie and Alan come to the rescue; Christo can stay with them three days a week.

So it's decided. We will move to Grassy after Christmas. Simple. Gives us plenty of time to get the house in order and pack while the agent advertises the place for rent.

Then: 'Mrs Nicholson, I've found some tenants for you, with really good references,' the agent warbles into my mobile late one afternoon. 'It's exactly what they're looking for and they are ready to sign a lease today. But there's a hitch. They want to be in before Christmas.'

'But that gives us less than three weeks.'

'Yes, I know, but good tenants are hard to find … '

The last time we moved, the company we both worked for was relocating from Melbourne to Sydney and everything was done for us. This time, the busiest time of year for removalists, it is going to be a nightmare. At least Alix is settled.

That night I'm on the internet, Googling around looking for companies offering online quotes until I find a firm that organises backloading and packing. I phone to lock in the date, 20 December.

'Oh, one more thing,' I explain to the helpful woman on the other end of the line. 'Our house at Grassy Head is at the top of a very steep drive. Perhaps you should let the driver know.'

'Thank you, dear. Yes, I will.'

The packers turn up and they're a delight, so quick and competent; the next day the backloader arrives. 'G'day,' he says, stony faced. 'This it?' He wanders from room to room sizing up the load, a man in his fifties who has the worries of the world on his shoulders judging by the frown lines on his face.

He doesn't seem overjoyed at what he sees. 'Jeez. You've gotta lotta stuff.' Shakes his head. 'My back is buggered,' he mutters. 'Gotta get out of this game.'

In an effort to brighten his day, I ask if there's anything I can do. A cup of coffee? A cold drink? He grimaces dispiritedly and calls in his team, two young Irish travellers, one of whom has hurt his leg and needs to sit down frequently, and another who can stay for only two hours. Aching and limping and checking their watches, the trio painfully load up the dented old truck outside.

Meanwhile Christo is preparing to leave Bondi Junction at the same time as the movers so he'll be at Grassy when they get there, ETA 8 pm.

As the truck of happy wanderers pulls away, Christo drives off behind them, our vehicle jam-packed with paraphernalia. On the passenger's side in the front is the veena my mother brought back from Malaysia for me, as hand luggage, in the early 1970s.

The veena is a stringed instrument, about my height, a relative of the sitar. It has been everywhere with me since then, although I have no idea how to play it. The wide brass frets are held in place with black wax that melted somewhere on its way across the Tasman when Christo and I moved to Auckland in 1989; the wax then hardened. The frets are in slightly different positions now one string has broken and the others are dusted with rust. They tell me a veena in good condition can fetch about $4000 these days.

By night-time I'm feeling somewhat sorry for myself in the empty house, and definitely not looking forward to sleeping on the floor in a borrowed swag. Well, at least I'm exhausted after days of touching up paint on the walls, dusting the timber blinds and cleaning kitchen cupboards. So maybe I'll sleep. I've kept the telly for company, and watch some reality drivel while I devour a Portuguese chicken burger (with chilli).

Christo rings at 7.45 pm to let me know he's at Grassy.

An hour passes. Uncomfortable as I am, my eyes are starting to close.

The shrill ring of the phone wakes me at 10.45 pm. 'They've just called on the mobile. They're on Grassy Head Road and I'm going down to meet them.'

'But it's so late. When on earth are they going to unpack?'

'Blowed if I know. Listen, love. Gotta go. I'll call when it's all done.'

Guiltily, I curl up on the swag and drift off to a re-run of a Sylvester Stallone movie. Christo's next call comes at 1.30 am. 'They've gone.'

'That was quick.'

'Ah, yes.' I can hear in his wry tone that there's more to come. 'The truck couldn't get up the hill so I've helped them unload it all into the packing shed. I hope Greg doesn't want to get in there tomorrow.'

'What! Are you okay? How are we going to get all the stuff up to the house?'

'Well, babe, I guess I'll get as much as I can into our truck and carry the rest up.'

'You can't do all that on your own. You'll kill yourself.' But that indeed is what he does: queen-size bed ensemble, bags of old toys, paintings, garden tools, table and chairs, my rug loom, boxes of books, computer, kitchen appliances ...

But at least we are in, four days before Christmas. Not that we're going to be able to have Christmas here; our life is in boxes in the Grassy garage.

Our long-suffering friends the Bears say they'll put us up, and Alix suggests we have Christmas Day at her flat as Hayley will be away.

'Mum, you can't possibly unpack up there in time and it would be kind of nice to have Christmas at my place.' Christo, who's been desperately trying to get some order into the house, is delighted when I ring him with the news that we have a place to stay and a plan for Christmas Day.

'Sounds terrific,' he says. He sounds exhausted.

'Before you come back to Sydney,' I tell him, 'would you ask Greg if you can pick some of the Christmas bush for Kerrie?'

Christmas Eve with the Bears and their other friends is a tradition we've enjoyed with them since we returned from Melbourne in 1997. Everyone brings an offering (this time, it'll be rhubarb-red armfuls of Christmas bush from us), Christo joins the carol-singing in the front room and I bah-humbug in the jasmine-scented courtyard with anyone else who's had enough of good old King Wenceslas.

Alix has begged us to have our usual Christmas Day ritual too, so we turn up early in the morning with boxes of food and gifts. Strawberries (and cream for us girls), followed by bacon and eggs for brunch, then presents, then the lemon turkey stuffing I've made every year since 1980 — a specialty of our foodie mate Linda.

I start rummaging in Alix's cupboards. 'Where are your herbs, darling? I need marjoram and thyme.'

'Mum, I'm a student. I have to live on instant noodles most of the time. I don't have anything like herbs.'

So I send husband and daughter out to find what I need, crumbling the bread into chunks, grating lemon zest, slopping in some white wine, adding an egg and mixing the lot in the big old bowl my father used for bread-making.

I enjoy preparing the festive meal by myself and, when they return, laughing and joking, it doesn't matter that they have only been able to find mixed herbs.

'That'll be fine,' I tell them, pushing the aromatic stuffing under the skin of the turkey with my fingers before cramming the baking dish into Alix's small oven. One final check to see that the summer berry pudding I made the night before is still upright in the fridge, and then it's off to Alix's lounge room to watch videos for a couple of hours as the pedestal fan swings valiantly left and right to dispel the heat.

'Turkey's ready,' I call, and we squeeze in around her low coffee table to eat lashings of hot roast dinner on a roasting hot Sydney day. The perfect Nicholson family Christmas.

Back in Grassy, Mum arrives, horn tooting, for a ten-day stay.

'Oh, Gilly. Just as beautiful as I remember,' she announces, edging herself slowly out from behind the driver's wheel. Her only real health complaint is bursitis in one hip, and general stiffness.

'What, me or the view?'

'You of course, darling.' Her laugh is deep and full of affection.

Peering into the station wagon, I see the back seats are down and the boot is crammed with boxes. 'God, what's all that, Mum?'

'My painting gear. I'm hoping you'll let me use the potting shed for a project I'm working on.'

'Yeah, sure.'

'Well, just leave them in the car for now and we'll unpack all that stuff tomorrow.'

I help her inside with her suitcase and ask, 'Is it time for a whisky?'

'You bet.' She knows we don't always have some at home and brings her own, in case.

'Well, you pour it then. I won't get it right.'

She likes hers with water, Dad liked his whisky with ice and I learned early on that every serious Scotch drinker has their individual preference.

'So what's this project you're working on?'

'Matisse.' He's one of her favourite painters. 'I have about forty square boards prepared and on each one I'm going to paint sections of Matisse paintings, close-ups if you like, in different proportions. When I finish, I'd like to have an exhibition … Pieces of Matisses.'

Mum sips her whisky. 'What do you think?'

What do I think? I think I have a remarkable mother. She's the one who led me here.

chapter seven

'When we speak of Nature, it is wrong
to forget that we are ourselves part of
Nature. We ought to view ourselves with
the same curiosity and openness with
which we study a tree, the sky or a
thought, because we too are linked
to the entire universe.'

Henri Matisse

February is incredibly hot and still, and I long for autumn. Even with the ceiling fans going and windows and doors open my skin is slick with sweat all day, and the fact that I am going through the longest menopause in the history of womankind doesn't help.

Sunshine glares through a covering of light grey cloud that melts into the horizon, barely visible beyond the sea haze. Behind Yarrahapinni, a tantalising slab of dark green-grey cloud hovers broodingly as if pondering its path, tail disappearing westwards. 'Keep coming,' I say to it. 'We need the rain.' Even here there is drought. Greg's had to get the pump going to water the bananas.

Bindi's in the greenhouse, digging deeply into one of the long sand pits for relief. I still don't understand the design of this structure and feel ashamed that, even though almost a year has passed, nothing grows there except a low, wandering weed with heart-shaped leaves, the occasional cobbler's peg and a tenacious plant with hairy leaves and tiny white flowers that I daren't disturb in case it's something precious. I try to imagine the greenhouse when Brian was here, filled with anthuriums, their dramatic red flowers in brilliant profusion.

The dog looks up as I come out on the back porch, but my presence isn't enough to entice her from her cool spot. I call hello to her but stay put under the eaves, hoping for a trickle of breeze.

I don't know how Greg can work in this weather, but he does four or five days a week and sometimes at weekends, bagging newly formed bunches of bananas or cutting down those ready for packing. Sometimes I see him in the distance, humping bunches that can weigh up to 50 kilograms up the hill to his ute.

The thought of Christo and I taking on the role of banana farmers, I realise, really is out of the question. It's not just the heavy physical work of carrying bananas; there's fertilising and spraying to be done, and the shallow-rooted plants need to be propped up with tall stakes to help support their swelling loads of fruit. Working all the time on rocky, often slippery slopes at an angle of 40 degrees.

I've been dipping into *The Queensland Agricultural and Pastoral Handbook Volume II*, Fruit and Vegetables, Second Edition (1961). My father's. Years after he died in 1977 from cancer, I spied its green hardback in Mum's bookshelves and took it as a memento. Now I thumb through it as I saw him do time after time, and it's coming in handy, despite being out of date. In any case, it is all I have to work with as I try to glean what's involved in farming bananas before we finally decide on their fate — and ours.

One particular sentence about harvesting tall banana varieties grabs my attention … 'a slanting cut is made halfway through the pseudostem at a suitable height. This allows the plant to sag sideways and the "tail" or flower end of the bunch may be caught and used to guide the bunch down until it can be cut easily. In either operation, two men should work together.'

Two men, huh? As each sweltering hour goes by I am more and more convinced that we can't do this. Farming bananas doesn't sound like fun at all.

Dizzy has just been around to engage Bindi in a quick rumble, which means Greg must be working quite close to the house today. I haven't seen him, but I've heard the occasional distinctive thud his machete makes as he drops another bunch of bananas.

'You there, Greg?' I call down into the maze of bananas on the mountainside.

A head appears from behind a thatch of banana leaves, followed by a waving hand; Greg was up a ladder, bagging. Diz and Bindi rush up to him, tongues dripping — they don't enjoy the heat either.

Trudging from the steamy plantation, Greg is drenched in sweat. 'How you going?'

He drags a small container from his pocket and sprays his arms and legs. 'Bloody paper wasps. They're everywhere. I've used two cans of this stuff today and they're still attacking me.'

'Can I make you a coffee? Get you a cold drink?'

'No thanks, mate. Once I stop I won't want to go back in there.' But he seems happy to have a chat. I admit I enjoy yarning with Greg. He's intelligent, interesting and, without even trying, he's teaching me a lot.

'What've you been up to?' he asks, slapping at a March fly with his hat. It's not March yet, but the flies don't know it; they've been around since last October.

'Nothing much. Writing a bit. Christo's working in Sydney three days a week now.'

'Yeah, I thought I hadn't seen him for a while. What are you writing?'

'Magazine stuff. Human interest stories mostly.'

Not that I intend to do it for much longer. The good stories are too often sad ones, and I find myself getting too close to the suffering of other people. Strangely, as I get older I find it increasingly difficult to shield myself emotionally as I suck out the intimate details of lives less fortunate.

I interview a breathless teenage girl with cystic fibrosis, who pleads for the body parts she needs to go on living ('If it's too late for me, maybe someone else will be moved by my story'). She needs a donor, someone her size, of compatible blood type, with healthy lungs, heart, kidneys in the next few weeks or … The story is not quite newsy enough to make it into print before she dies.

I take it hard. Some tough investigative journo I turned out to be.

'Hey, Greg, while I've got you … the bananas on the other side of the house aren't looking too good. Are they all right?'

'Nah, I've given them the needle. Those bananas have never been very good.' He walks with me up to the crest and we gaze at the dying bananas, their long leaves drooping brownly around their ankles like crisp petticoats. Weeds have started to move in between their slumped carcases, showing robust and green as they claim the space the bananas are vacating.

Where there was a forest of bananas blocking the view down the slope, now I can see trees. Not natives. At least, not wattles. I've come to recognise those now and feel a childlike sense of pride. Greg says the trees are self-sown avocados, not much good for eating because they're more stone than fruit. I'd have to be convinced, though, an avocado is an avocado and if they're hanging off the tree I'm not going to leave them to rot.

Among the avos, I spot some pink and white lantana flowers; the dreaded milk vine is snaking its way up a tall tree stump, cloaking it in pale green. Bugger.

'The best bananas are the ones I planted over there,' he tells me, indicating a slope on the far side of the property just above my dam, neat rows forming a pretty patchwork.

Then Greg swings his gaze back to the dying bananas.

'Did you know you've got phytophthora?'

'Pardon?'

'See that avo, how its leaves are yellow? That's phytophthora. It's in that other one over there too.'

But to my city-trained eyes, the leaves on every tree I can see look green. I'm embarrassed to ask Greg the obvious question, but I want to know.

'Er … what's phy … ?' I don't have a hope of pronouncing it.

'Phytophthora. Root rot. Those trees are dying.'

The only sick plants I can pick out are the bananas Greg's given 'the needle'.

'How does it work? Can you stop it?'

'If it's in the soil, you can't get rid of it and it spreads to other trees. Myself, I wouldn't worry too much about saving those seed avos, they're not worth it. But some people reckon if you cut the trees right back they can come good.'

How far back is back? Well, Christo has an axe and a saw. Maybe the metal blade of the brushcutter …

'Best thing to do if you want to keep them is give them the needle.'

I am more puzzled than ever. 'Um … but you said you gave the bananas the needle to kill them?'

Greg explains. You inject chemical solutions into the stem of plants depending on the problem: to kill bananas you use biologically sensitive glyphosate, whereas potassium phosphonate solution helps reverse the effect of phytophthora root rot. There's special injection equipment to make either job easy, he says.

Neither sounds easy to me. Thankfully we won't have to kill off the bananas when Greg goes, he's said he'll do that. But phytophthora? Is everything on the hillside going to turn yellow and die? So much to learn (and so little time, my rueful side adds).

Later, while the word phytophthora is imprinted on my consciousness, I log onto the internet to find out more. *Phytophthora cinnamoni* is soil-borne, too small to see without a microscope, it affects introduced and native species, often kills its host because the diseased roots can't absorb water, becomes active in hot, wet conditions, loves avocados and bananas, travels on boots or tyres that have picked up infected soil, as well as being transported in running water, and this very damaging and resilient pathogen can live in the soil and dead plants for several years.

Bloody hell. Phytophthora has found an ideal home right here.

This is ridiculous. Here we are sitting on the veranda, hot and uncomfortable in the late afternoon, and staring at the Pacific Ocean. 'For Pete's sake, let's go for a swim,' I say to Christo.

'We're not taking the dog,' he warns me.

'No, of course not.' Dogs aren't allowed on Grassy's main beach without a leash anyway.

My skin is so tacky I need his help to drag on my Speedos, a stretchy one-piece affair I chose because it squishes most of my lumpy bits into a smooth, even plane. But it's so tight that I get all tangled up in it when I slip my arms through the shoulder straps.

'Thanks darling.' The mirror reassures me that nothing has escaped, nothing is wobbling. It's okay to be seen on the beach. But when we arrive at Grassy Head, people are traipsing back to the reserve.

The board at the entrance to the sandy track reads: 'NE winds. Beach closed due to bluebottles'. Damn. I really need to cool off.

'Want to try Scotts Head?' Christo asks.

'Good idea. But can we have a look at Grassy first? We haven't been down here for ages.'

'Speak for yourself,' he says, eyebrows lifting mockingly above his hazel eyes. Wish I could do that eyebrow thing.

Yes, I haven't been here for ages but Christo runs along the beach most mornings when he's at Grassy.

The short walk along the sandy trail curves upward through a sparse forest of coastal banksias, waking my calf muscles immediately to the task of plodding through the deep drift of sand.

We break out of the bush to a heavenly, salt-laden wind and pounding breakers. Grassy isn't quite deserted: a young couple lying half-hidden in the dunes exploring the chemistry of love, and there are boys clambering up the almost-vertical path to the top of Grassy. I make a mental promise to climb it myself one day. I am definitely getting fitter. (These days I can even raise my left knee high enough to get my leg into my knickers without leaning on something for support.)

Wild surf has dumped hundreds of bluebottles in tangles of poisonous tentacles, abandoning them on the high water line. Some of the wind-blown travellers still move slightly in the wind as their translucent pillow-shaped sails reach out for rescue, seeking tide and wind to set them on another rudderless voyage.

North-easterlies have brought them here, rolling them from wave to wave. Where from and where to, I wonder. The northern hemisphere, where they are identified much more appropriately as Portuguese men o' war? We tread the line of blue formed by the waves, poking and prodding … carefully. Although they are helpless, they can still deliver a nasty sting.

Occasionally we spot a different creature among the bluebottles: round, about the size of a 20-cent piece, with a fine fringe of iridescent blue tentacles. One side of the body is the inky blue of the tentacles, the other side the colour of sand.

'I think,' Christo says pensively, 'they are porpita. They're wind-blown, too, but I don't think they're poisonous. I can't tell you how I know that, but I must have read it somewhere.'

I wouldn't doubt him for a minute. He's a sponge for unusual information discovered in unlikely places … this is a man who learned how to scramble eggs in the pages of a Leslie Charteris novel. Why wouldn't he know these are porpita?

Christo pops a few bluebottles under his sandalled feet; it's almost irresistible, and so is the surf. Tentatively I wade out into the cool, green water up to my ankles, hoping that the stingers are all marooned behind me on the sand. But just 2 metres farther out, it's bluebottle soup. I think we'll swim at Scotts.

In many ways, Scotts Head is more spectacular than Grassy. From the road in, you look down on three beaches: two are small bays nestled between rocky outcrops, and the third and most popular stretches for several kilometres in the shelter of Scotts Head. At Grassy you can't see the beach until you go over the dunes.

The surf club, recreation hall and caravan park are right there beside the main beach, with a few shops on the opposite side of the road. It's a township with a cosy, comfy feel about it, but it's changing as newcomers discover it — and not for the better. The usual story: bland subdivisions, ostentatious contemporary homes staking claim to the oceanfront views, long-time residents facing alienation and higher council rates.

Still, we're here to swim, to wash away the heat of the day in the safe, clear waters of this dazzling beach. Aaaah. The water is quite still and I float on my back to look up to the clear blue sky. Then I close my eyes and bob with the waves, filling my ears with peace and pleasure. I could lie here for ever, forgetting my worries, letting wind and waves transport me.

Distantly, I hear a voice. It's Christo. I fold in the middle, let myself sink to the sand and surface with eyes blinking. 'Gotta go, love. The beach is closing … bluebottles.' Wouldn't you know?

I don't like the look of the wasps (or hornets, or whatever they are) flying around our veranda, especially after Greg's experiences with the paper wasps. Big buggers these are, black and orange. Menacing. So far none has landed on me, but there must be a dozen hanging around and they come too close for my liking. The house was pristine when we moved in, but now there are cocoon-shaped mud nests in the cornices outside and around the windows.

I'm not scared exactly, but I do not want them here buzzing near me. What should I do? Dad used to smoke them out, I think, always in the evening, then destroy the nests. Will they chase me if I disturb them? Maybe I'll wait until Christo gets back and we'll deal with them together …

Whatever they are, they're in the garage too. When I throw up the roller door, I see them moulded into its recesses. And there are more in the potting shed … on a piece of shade cloth, on the rafters, tucked in beside the light switch …

Enough of this. I'm going to deal with them tonight. I make a torch from tightly rolled newspaper, a bit too tightly at first. It won't light, so I re-roll it. Beside me are the broom and a bucket of water for dousing the torch. The screen door is open so I can get inside quickly if they chase me. I can't see any flying around, so hopefully they're in their nests.

I choose a nest near the door, standing as far away from it as I can with the smoking torch. I don't want to blister the paintwork … or have far to run. Nothing happens. I give it half a minute. Still nothing.

Okay. Torch in the bucket. The smoke must have done its job. Nevertheless, with visions of being attacked by an unseen swarm I find I'm trembling as I bring up the broom handle to whack the silent nest. Bang. I hit the wall and miss the nest entirely. Oh shit. I calm myself down and try again. Slide the broom handle up the wall, across the nest and … splat. Bull's eye. Dropping the broom I dash inside and close the door. Not a sound except my thudding heart. I peer out. The nest lies shattered on the ground, a dead spider and a whitish grub among the shards. Nothing is trying to attack me.

I felt the fear and did it anyway.

Months later, it occurs to me to check out the CSIRO website. This is what I find. A detailed photograph of a slender black orange-banded mud wasp, often wrongly called a hornet, that makes a nest of mud or clay on rock faces and buildings. 'Mud wasps are solitary in habit — the nest is constructed by only one female wasp ... Typically, the mother wasp catches a particular kind of insect or spider, stings and paralyses it, carries it back and places it in the nest, lays an egg on it and seals the nest ... Female mud wasps are not aggressive and stings rarely happen.'

Monday is rubbish night. When Grassy was more like our holiday home, we could deal with the small amount of household garbage but now we're filling one of our three wheelie bins every week.

Putting it out for collection means driving the smelly bin to the bottom of the road. Ugh. What if the lid falls open and the garbage spills out? Some locals leave their bins permanently on Grassy Head Road, but we don't like the idea of making the road look ugly, so before Christo returns to Sydney on Sunday he loads up the grey bin and devises an intricate arrangement with stretchy octopus straps to keep the lid closed. He'll drop it off on his way.

I walk down on Tuesday afternoon, with Bindi on the lead so she doesn't do a runner, to move the bin out of sight; Christo will pick it up on Wednesday night when he comes past. But when I get to it, I find it's still full of garbage. The other bins have been emptied, why ... ? I look around helplessly. What am I going to do?

Michael, the bloke who runs a fruit tree nursery near us, is waiting for the school bus to deposit his children. 'Could be your bin's the wrong colour,' he suggests. 'Green is the colour of Kempsey Shire bins and they won't take other colours. The grey bins are from Nambucca.'

What? Grey bins? Green bins? What does the colour matter? I'll call the council. Bindi and I trudge back along the dusty road and up the hill.

Now, while my sister's the mayor and everyone knows that, even though I haven't whispered a word, not knowing how the political land lies, I don't feel it's right to try to use my family connection. So I don't phone Janet, but ring the appropriate department about my problem.

'Yes, it's correct that we're not supposed to pick up garbage in a Nambucca Shire bin,' the polite voice of a young woman tells me. 'But you say you're new to the area. Let me just check to see if everything is in order with your rates to make sure we haven't made a mistake.'

Still very courteous, she is obviously reading from a computer screen in front of her. 'Your rates are up to date but you don't seem to have paid the fee for garbage services.'

'The rates don't cover rubbish collection?'

'That's right. To have your rubbish collected you need to pay an extra fee of $2 a week.'

'I didn't know that. So what am I supposed to do? My husband is in Sydney, the bin is full of rotting garbage and I have no way of getting it back up our drive, which is 2 kilometres away from the main road.'

Very, very nicely. 'I'm sorry, Mrs Nicholson. You can take your garbage to the council tip if you like. It costs about the same on a weekly basis as the council's annual fee.'

'But I don't have a car.' Anxious and annoyed, I hang up with an abrupt thank you.

Now it's time to call the mayor.

'Settle, petal,' is Janet's unsympathetic response.

'But what am I going to do with the bin?'

Big sigh. 'Just move it for now so it's not causing a nuisance. Christo can take it to the tip when he gets back.'

'How come the rates don't cover the rubbish collection? In Sydney they do. And the rates we pay there are the same as we pay here.'

Very patiently, this is how she explains it. Regional councils have their populations spread over a wider area, often having to duplicate services, yet they don't have as many ways to collect revenue as the city councils. No parking meters, for instance. As for the rates, state government pegs them.

'So you can pay the council to collect your rubbish, or go to the tip. Don't give me a hard time about rates; I've got troubles of my own. Geese in Riverside Park.'

'What? What geese? What are you talking about?'

'Haven't you been reading the paper?'

'No. Tell me. Where's Riverside Park?'

'Riverside Park is the park in Kempsey alongside the river. There are geese there, and they breed. We've had complaints from people that they have attacked children and that there are so many of them now that they shit everywhere and make a terrible mess where people want to have picnics and so on. So council is moving them.

'Meanwhile there are a few people who want them to stay, they reckon they're part of the park's appeal. And one person has accused council of killing the geese, which is bloody rubbish. I've been getting anonymous threats, would you believe, and people ringing me at home abusing me.'

'You're kidding. Are you okay?'

'Well, it's not been a great week exactly, but it won't get on top of me. Now you can understand why I'm a wee bit preoccupied.'

Who'd be a mayor?

I'm fed up with waiting for the piles of Rhodes grass to break down; the whole thing looks like a dried-out mess, nothing like compost. Even though the weather should be sending those earthworms and bacteria into a chewing frenzy, there's no evidence of biological change.

Bugger it. I'll turn it again. If that doesn't work I'll forget about it. One day it will compost down I suppose.

The pads of grass are heavy so I try forking smaller amounts each time before turning them over; much easier, but without the weight the grass tends to spill off the fork and I have to hold the pile in place with my hand.

Soon I develop a rhythm: fork under the grass, hand on top, turn. But it's so hot that within minutes I have to stop and rest. I lean on the fork regarding my handiwork when I see a sudden movement in the pile of grass I've just turned … oh, God, a snake, a brown snake.

'Christo!' I shriek, frozen in fear. 'Christo!' He's in the house, I know he is. 'Christo-o!' The snake has vanished and there's no need for me to be frightened, but even so I want him here. 'Christo-o-o-o!'

At last he materialises on the back porch. 'What's up? You okay?'

'A brown snake. God. I almost touched it … A snake.'

He moves towards me. 'Stay still. Where is it?'

'Gone.'

He comes closer. 'Where?'

'Well, it came out just there and it went over there.'

Concerned husband. 'Can't see anything now, babe. How big was it?'

'Er, not very big I suppose, about 30 centimetres, but it came out just here near me and it was in my mulch piles and I didn't have gloves on and … '

Christo pulls me into his shoulder and kisses the back of my neck. 'You must have been terrified,' he says caringly, and I feel him trying to stifle his laughter as he hides his face in my hair.

chapter eight

'Koalas in NSW now occur mainly on the north coast and are uncommon, rare or extinct in other parts of the State … Koalas feed almost exclusively on the leaves of a small number of trees, mostly eucalypts. In any one area, only a few types of trees are favoured as the main food source.'

Natural Resource Management Advisory Series:
Note 9, Department of Environment and Conservation (NSW)

Mick is coming down from Gympie for the fishing, which he reckons is better in autumn, and to help Christo turn the small shed near the Christmas bush into a chook house. It's going to be an interesting visit. Mick is my 'little' sister Kathleen's first husband — a very smart guy, an old rock'n'roller and the father of her two eldest kids, Eloise and Errin. I was a witness at their registry office wedding in Sydney in the 1970s, Kathleen wearing a floral print dress she had sewn, and dimpled blonde toddler Eloise in one to match.

The ceremony was simple, the small party at their Kings Cross flat a lot of fun. At one point I remember laughing so much my sides ached. It was the last time I smoked dope. Funny that.

We've always liked Mick but lost touch with him once he and Kath separated and the kids grew up, but Eloise has kept us updated. Mick moved to Townsville and completed a double major in chemistry, worked in Outback Queensland selling farm machinery of some kind and then moved down to Gympie to live on a bushland property.

In all the years they were apart — throughout Kathleen's second marriage, the birth of two more daughters, Sophia and Nina, and her second divorce — Eloise was certain her parents would get back together. 'Dad says she's the only woman he's ever loved,' she would tell everyone. 'It'll happen. You'll see.'

And somehow it did. Mind you, I don't know how and probably never will. Anyway, it's really none of my business.

In preparation for the trip, Mick's been on the phone to Christo, asking for measurements of the old shed we're converting for the hens. Has Christo got any sheets of tin? Spare timbers? An old door? How far away is the power source?

Mick arrives in his ute with most of what he needs, including a used timber-framed screen door, chainsaw, circular saw, petrol-driven generator and boxes of mystery tools and supplies. He's been camping and fishing along the way.

'Good to see ya, Mick,' Christo says, extending a hand.

'Likewise,' he replies.

'Cuppa tea?'

'Yeah. That'd go down well. I'll just bring my things in first. Now I don't know if you've been told, but you'll have to speak up a bit. I'm deaf in one ear and the other one is going. Too much wild living,' he finishes with an impish grin I remember well; it hasn't aged along with his hairline.

Christo is hanging over the back of the ute checking out what Mick's brought with him. 'Honey, that's what we need next. A chainsaw. And a generator.'

'Chainsaws are dangerous. I don't want you to have one.' (This advice to the most safety-conscious person I know.)

'There'll be times when we need a chainsaw, to cut wood for the fire, for example. What if a tree falls and we need to get past it? We can't live in the bush and not have the tools, love.'

At least he's given up on the idea of shotgun, which he used to trot out when we first came to Grassy.

'Well, I guess you're right about a chainsaw. But what about the generator? Why do we need that? We've managed without one so far.'

'Power. We've already had a couple of blackouts. If we had a generator we'd have light and be able to keep the fridge going.'

That's true. Everything in the house is electric.

Christo's not finished yet. 'A generator also comes in handy when you have to do a job that's nowhere near a power point. Like sawing through timber, which is what Mick's going to be doing down at the shed.'

I guess he's right, but all these things are so expensive.

'I don't want to make you angry but,' he continues, 'while we're on the subject ... we could also use a fire pump before next summer. Although the area around our house is clear of trees, look at all the bush around us. And we are going to have to have a tractor or at the very least a substantial ride-on mower or we'll never be able to keep this place under control.'

I'm doing sums in my head. The cost, the cost. If we get a tractor, it's going to have to be new because we don't have the knowledge, or the tools, to deal with any breakdowns.

'I dunno, darling. Can we talk about it later? Sorry, Mick.' But he's busy unloading, humming a Bob Dylan song, oblivious.

Over a couple of beers or three at dusk, we catch up and, while I cook dinner, the boys play CDs and talk Rolling Stones and the blues. Mick picks up Christo's latest guitar, a steel-fronted number, and strums it nostalgically. He's played guitar all his life — now he can't hear well enough to be sure he's in tune. The way it goes, says Mick.

Next morning, we're going to burn off a huge pile of weeds, rotten timber and prunings we've amassed in the centre of the big yard. Fire bans have been lifted, we've alerted neighbours and the fire service and we're ready to go. Looking forward to it.

Mick squats comfortably 50 metres from the pile in the shade of one of our errant mango trees, drawing on a rollie. 'I think it might be an idea to wet around the pile,' he says, matter-of-factly. Christo already has the hose nearby and nods. He soaks the ground thoroughly.

'There's no wind now, but it could come up pretty fast on this hill,' Mick adds, as Christo sets match to buried firelighters.

Whoosh! In three seconds the pile is swallowed in flames that leap to twice its height, singeing a few of Greg's bananas, leaves curling blackly. Uh-oh. The speed and violence of the fire shock me; the heat sends me staggering backwards. Although Christo is working the hose constantly, the flames climb higher and higher, scattering burning pieces of vegetation. I watch horrified as the fire takes on a will of its own, the speed of it making me feel ill. Hurry up, I command the fire. Die down.

Eventually the fire reaches its peak, but debris is still whirling away. I follow every piece with my eyes, watching it nervously until it expires. At last, almost as quickly as it leapt into life, the conflagration subsides to a glowing red heap. We have been very, very lucky.

'Good fire,' Mick calls out, grinning. 'Bit close to the bananas, but.'

Christo has to go back to Sydney, so I'm Mick's offsider for the chook house project the next day. 'Well, Gillian? Ready to give me a hand?' Bindi and I troop down to where he's parked the ute and neatly laid out all manner of tools. He's been up since sparrow's he tells me, and has dug trenches about 20 centimetres deep right around the shed.

'I'll put you on the circular saw to cut these banana props to length.'

'I don't know how to use it.'

The lengths of timber are set out on two sawhorses (Mick's, of course). Mick picks up the saw's cord, plugs it into an extension lead and walks over to the generator. Flicking the switch, he smiles at me. 'Well, I'm about to show you how. Watch carefully.'

He demonstrates; he's obviously an old hand.

'Your turn. Don't hurt yourself.'

Concentrating on the pencil lines he's marked, I gingerly position the saw against the timber stake and, with Mick steadying it, press the starter button. Pink sawdust flies to the whine of the saw and it's done, just like that. Slightly crooked but not bad.

'That'll do 'er,' Mick says, arranging another stake across the sawhorses. In five minutes, all the stakes are cut to size — and I have a new skill.

Next, we cut lengths of wire netting with Mick's tin snips; they're to be fixed with horseshoe nails to the stakes.

'Here's another job for you while I do some thinking,' Mick tells me.

'But I've never really used a hammer ... except to remove nails.'

'Well, you can start learning. You might hit your thumb a few times, so be careful.' The trick, I discover, is keeping the U-nails straight as you strike them. I try holding them with thumb and forefinger, which leaves too little of the nail exposed and raises the risk of giving my thumb a hammering. Then I experiment by sandwiching the nail between forefinger and middle finger, but I can't get a firm-enough grip.

Mick is contemplating the space where the door's going to be, and I'm aware of his sideways glances and barely concealed smile.

I decide on the thumb and forefinger method. 'Yow,' I yell with my first decent blow.

'Told ya to be careful. Don't want Christo having a go at me when he gets back.'

'Mick, it hurts.'

'Well, just take things slowly. We're not in a rush.' Pain is a great teacher. Before long, I have the technique mastered (although at least half the nails are askew) and the mesh lengths attached to the stakes.

We roll the mesh around the stakes a couple of times and place them lengthwise in the trenches. Rocks and soil go on top. No foxes will get into this chook house once we've nailed the mesh over the corrugated iron walls.

By the time Christo's back on Wednesday night, the job is almost complete. The screen door, with its scrolled ironwork feature, is a masterpiece. I'm tempted to paint it.

'I thought I'd cook dinner tonight,' Mick announces. 'I'll be heading off tomorrow. Got any peanut oil?'

He spends three hours in the kitchen preparing a wonderfully spicy stir-fry, and over a few beers afterwards he tells us he's keen to get back up north. 'Missing Kathleen, huh?' I'm fishing, hoping for better results than he has had at the beach that day.

He smiles enigmatically. 'Well, you might say that. Then again, you might say she's missing me.' He drags on his fag and then laughs.

'You'll have to finish off a couple of things at the chook house,' he tells Christo. 'You need to patch a couple of holes with wire netting.'

'That's fine, mate. No worries. Can't thank you enough for what you've done.'

'I enjoyed it. You know, I've been thinking about that blaze you two started. What if I was to build you a fire pit lined with rocks? You've got more than enough of them around here. It'd be nice sitting around a fire at night, keep the mozzies away. And you could burn off in it without scaring the shit out of your neighbours. Next time I'm down, I'll collect a few nice rocks.'

Mick gets away early the next day, a bottle of Bundy rum from us hidden under the passenger's seat to thank him. We're going to miss him, and I hope with all my heart that things work out for him and Kathleen (and, of course, Eloise!). It's good having him back in the family.

One night we get a call from Pam and Phillip, a lovely English couple whose house we rented in Queens Park when we arrived in Sydney from Melbourne. Since then they've become good friends. P and P stayed at Grassy and minded the dog last weekend while we were in Sydney.

'Thank you for letting us stay,' says Phil. 'Pam and I had an absolutely wonderful time, absolutely wonderful, but something a bit odd happened. I don't know quite where to start. There was this fellow who came round to inspect the property, said it was something to do with surveying the place for the rates assessment. We were a bit suspicious at first, but he gave us his card, which seems legitimate. We've kept it for next time we see you.'

'I'm sure it's okay, Philip. Don't worry.'

'Well, it's not that we think he was up to something. It's you see, I'm trying to explain that, well, your place is so secluded and we didn't hear him arrive and we were outside … sunbaking, you see.'

I had forgotten. Pam and Phillip are a very fit, lithe, tanned couple … and naturists. Naked baby boomers must have been a first for the surveyor. Maybe he'll ring before coming next time.

Everyone who visits is impressed with our greenhouse complex, pointing out that we could grow just about anything there. Of course, pretty well all our visitors are like us — full of great ideas and absolutely no practical advice how to go about it. One thought is to grow tomatoes, while someone suggests raising cycads until they're big enough to sell for a higher price than we paid. Anthurium flowers fetch a reasonable price, apparently, although I suspect when Brian was growing them he did it simply for the joy it gave him. As for the orchids Brian left us, they're not faring too well, despite the fact that everything I have read reiterates that they are easy to grow. Still, just when I think they're dying of neglect, a show of colour appears from the spear-like leaves to deliver a beautiful surprise. Sheer good luck, though.

The two nursery buildings look quite bleak; weeds are as high as the benches that remain almost empty. I can't decide what to grow, but I've bought two hundred black plastic pots just in case I'm inspired. I did find a clump of small bromeliads growing near the septic tank, separated them and arranged them in rows on a bench along one shady wall. But they just sat there, week after week doing nothing, before each finally produced a single bract of lavender flowers tipped with purple. Their name, matchstick bromeliads, describes them exactly — except that the matchsticks that grow at right angles to the stem (or whatever it is) bottlebrush style are only 2 or 3 centimetres long.

'Why don't you sell them at local markets?' suggests my mate Rosie.

'Because there's no money in it,' I reply.

'How do you know that?'

I've done the sums, I tell her. Besides these broms are very common. No one would want them.

Rosie announces she has come here to weed.

'Rosie, there's nearly 8 hectares here,' I tell her, laughing.

'Yes, I know, but I'm going to start at the house and work outwards.'

Every day she's out in the yard, poking around, looking at things and occasionally plucking at a cobbler's peg or thistle. As well as teaching me how not to weed, Rosie makes me laugh.

She's also a keen birdwatcher. From time to time, she points one out and names it: some that I think are swallows

— glossy brown-black feathers glistening as they dart erratically around the tree tops scooping fat insects from the air — she says are swifts. The small freckled birds that can barely lift themselves from the ground when they see Bindi coming, fluttering about as gracefully as a panicked chook, are quail.

'And you've got a couple of bush turkeys building a nest behind the packing shed. Though I'm surprised Bindi hasn't chased them away.'

Rosie is staying in the guest room we call the Mountain View Room (or Mum's room, when she's here), because it faces Yarrahapinni. From the window, the yard slopes down past the lemon and lemonade trees to a track that separates us from Mark's place, where Sally wattles have created a canopy of shade to deny the weeds further purchase.

But the most prominent item visible from the Mountain View Room is the grey concrete septic tank. No doubt it's in the right place, but what an eyesore. I've planted three lavender bushes in front of it and, after a shaky start, they're bushing out at last, bringing bees to taste its aromatic flower heads.

Yarrahapinni was once a significant Aboriginal site. Back in the 1980s, someone had the foresight to record the memories of a Nambucca Heads man, the late Harry 'Tiger' Buchanan, who told the story of the Yarrahapinni legend.

According to the legend, three clever men arrived at Scotts Head one day from across the sea and, as they walked up the beach, the water followed them, creating the first wave. The youngest went back down to the beach to see if the wave would follow him again; it did. The third time, he challenged the sea: 'Come on — see if you can catch me!' But he became trapped, so turned himself and his friends to stone. They escaped through a tunnel that led to two mountains — Yarrahapinni, the larger, and Bald Mountain.

Then they changed into a koala, or 'yarra' as the local Thungutti people say. Later, Yarra was killed by a Thungutti tribesman on top of the mountain, felled by a boomerang that cut the large creature into four. Pieces of the koala rolled down the mountainside, forming four large gullies where nothing grows to this day.

And as for koalas, they're dying out in New South Wales. Elsewhere, too.

From the Mountain View Room I notice a stand of tallowwood in the national park. If there are any koalas around here, that's where they'll be. I can only hope ... or could we plant tallow-wood at our place? Would that help? Australia without koalas ... it's incomprehensible.

Behind the African tulip tree is a guava, covered in golden fruit. I find their flavour too bland to be interesting but I can't see them go to waste, rotting on the ground. They also attract fruit fly because their skin is so easy to penetrate. I've offered some of the fruit to neighbours, but their reaction is like mine. Besides, guavas tend to self-seed around here; the birds love them as much as the fruit flies do.

I'll preserve them, that's what you do with a bumper harvest. I'll make guava jelly. I wash the fruit carefully (the skin is blotchy and you never know what might be on it) and place it in a large aluminium stockpot we bought at the Kempsey markets. The recipe I've unearthed in an old country-style cookbook calls for an awful lot of sugar, I think to myself. The mixture simmers away for hours before a test dollop of syrup sets quiveringly on a saucer so I know it's ready, and then I pour it into the sterilised jars I've been saving. What an accomplishment: eight bottles of homemade guava jelly. A bit sweet, but it's good. Shame we don't eat jam.

Although I miss Christo when he's away, his absence doesn't affect my sleeping. I'm not frightened on my own, and anyway, if strangers did turn up in the night, Bindi would certainly let me know. She loves the sound of her own voice so much she often goes over to Mark's and barks at the hillside, which sends an impressive echo back to her. She waits for the echo, and then barks again. Crazy dog. She'll never make a vicious guard dog — after an opening salvo of ferocious barks, she's more like to lick strangers to death than bite them.

After a lifetime of insomnia, here I always sleep well, lulled by the moon, the call of night birds, the dull drumming of the surf.

But one night at around 2 am, a far-off sound filters through my dreams. Drugged with sleep, I try to focus my senses. What? It sounds like a cow lowing. A cow? There aren't any cows. Think. Yes, cows at Margaret and Jim's. It lows again. Must be one of Jim and Margaret's cows or bulls or …

And again. A distressed, drawn-out cry. Is the animal hurt? Is it outside the house? There's no moonlight, and no cow that I can see from the bedroom window.

Bindi stretches lazily on her trampoline, yawns, and comes to my side as I stumble onto the veranda. It's chilly. Should have put on my robe. The cow calls again, sounding so alone and in pain I can't bear it. Bindi stands with me loyally but without any real interest. No matter how much I strain to peer through the night, there's nothing to see but the amorphous blackness of Jim and Margaret's native forest, swaying slightly in a cool breeze.

Back in bed, I burrow into the doona attempting to block out the awful noise, but sleep is impossible and I doze on and off until dawn.

At 8.30 am I call Margaret and Jim. 'G'day, Margaret, it's Gillian Nicholson. Hope I didn't wake you?'

'No, no. We've been up for quite a while.' Margaret always sounds cheerful.

'Margaret, I'm sorry to bother you, but could one of your cows have escaped?'

'Well, no, I don't think so. Why?'

So I explain about the cow, its cries of pain.

'Oh, oh yes. Not one of ours. It's a mother whose calf has been taken; it's crying.'

'That's terrible. It sounded so … heartbroken. It's one of the most sorrowful sounds I've ever heard.'

'Yes, it is awful. It's a fact of life, I'm afraid, but you never really get used to it.'

I can understand that.

On the scale of one to ten, I'd have to say my gardening-for-food performance rates about a five, considering the fruit trees were all established when we arrived. To be kind to myself, my whole working life has been defined by nine-to-five, annual holidays, in trays and out trays. But here, the deadlines are different. If you don't spray/fertilise/prune/mulch at the right times, you're buggered. Even if you know about all this stuff, which I don't, you've had it if the elements are really against you: seven days straight of heavy rain (or none for months), a plague of caterpillars, a broken leg … I'm just glad we're not farming for a living (yet, anyway).

I've improved the yield of the citrus, I reckon, and it looks as if we'll be eating oranges and grapefruit for breakfast any day now, having adopted Peter Cundall's passion for pruning. (I make Christo watch Peter Cundall on *Gardening Australia* with me. While Christo studied agriculture at high school in Tenterfield, not a lot of it stuck; for some reason, Latin was more his style.) I must attribute some of my success with citrus to fertilising, which I'm managing to do at more-or-less the correct times of year. Once, inadvertently, Christo and I both fertilised the trees within three weeks and it didn't seem to do them any harm.

The mango trees have been disappointing. In our first year, they were fabulous; last year we had not one mango. But Christo did enjoy pruning them. (Yes, he got his chainie.)

The two lychee trees have been prolific, producing masses of fruit each summer. But they're too tall to harvest, and most of the fruit is, of course, at the top. The pawpaw is heavy with promise and the fruit delicious — if I can get to it before the possums have sampled the ripe end.

Our biggest disappointment has been the stone fruit. I tell Christo growing stone fruit would be easier in colder climates where there is no fruit fly, but we are having a go. I've followed the diagrams in my *Yates Garden Guide* to shape the tree like a wine glass, a shape I am very familiar with, and the peach and nectarine bloom beautifully in the spring. We lost our first crops to fruit fly, the second to birds. Last summer, Greg lent us a net to keep the birds off, but somehow they found their way under it.

We have a fabulous macadamia nut tree but frankly, much as I love maccas, I don't have the enthusiasm or technique to crack the stone-hard shell and extract its sweetness. And there are two pecans, but they are way down near the pretty dam and we never remember to check them for nuts.

Vegies have been a mixed bag. I've succeeded with chillies without really trying, and my herbs all do really well. Rocket yes, cabbages and broccoli no. The zucchini actually succeeded when I thought they had failed; the yellow flowers kept failing to bear, and it was our neighbour Irene who told me, as I was about to reef them out, that the first flowers are male and to wait for the females. Got it! Beans have been wonderful, tomatoes too.

The potatoes are another story. At first I tried growing potatoes that had sprouted in my vegie bin, bunging them into deep soil and crossing my fingers. They produced a crop, but most of the spuds were riddled with calloused empty tunnels.

There are two items of food Christo cannot live without: bread (preferably white) and spuds (preferably mashed). He has perfected the art of mash, crafting it lovingly at least twice a week with garlic and shallots, and varying it sometimes by mashing it with pumpkin. So it's important that we get a potato patch going. And that means a visit to a produce store.

It's another world inside these barn-like places. Heady harvest smells of hay and straw, rows of gumboots, pelletised fertiliser and feed, chemicals to kill and cure everything, dog food in bags so big you almost need a trolley to shift them, seeds and irrigation supplies, backpacks for spraying. And many things we've never seen before.

'Got any seed potatoes?'

'Yeah. Over here. How many kilos do you want?' The shop assistant is poised over an enormous set of scales as Christo and I exchange glances. Kilos?

'I dunno, um … half a dozen?'

The shrivelled tubers tumble into the metal dish and three dollars later we're on our way home.

'We have to plant them on the shortest day of the year and harvest on the longest,' I tell Christo. 'I heard it on the local gardening program.'

'But it's not the winter solstice yet.'

'Don't worry. I'll keep them in a dark place in the garage until it's time. At least we've got 'em now and we can get the garden bed ready.'

We're old hands at this no-dig garden business now, and I reckon a thick top layer of straw will help keep the potatoes well covered. They mustn't be exposed to light while they're growing or they'll go green, which makes them toxic.

Three weeks later, we're ready. The towel covering the plastic bag of tubers to stop light getting in is exactly as I left it. I go to lift it off and my hand sinks into … nothing. I whip it off, magician-like. Hey, presto, the seed potatoes have vanished and, in their place, rat droppings. The cunning bastards have eaten them all without disturbing the towel or the plastic bag.

'Christo,' I wail. 'A rat's got your potatoes.' Ah well, I always enjoy a trip to the produce store.

chapter nine

'Roquefort is made from the milk of only one breed of sheep, it is made in only one place in France, and it is made in only one special way … Coke you can buy anywhere in the world and it is exactly the same.'

Mayor Philippe Folliot of St Pierre-de-Trevisy, population 610, quoted in 1999 in *The Washington Post*

Mid-autumn brings buttery, mellow days that unfold lazily before quickly melting into evening. The mild chill that dispels summer's humid pressure is a pleasant relief, and I'm looking forward to my birthday in May, even though it takes me a step closer to my sixtieth in a couple of years. We haven't had any rain for weeks, and the wide open azure skies are empty of clouds except for occasional hedges of cumulus lingering over the sea.

Anzac Day has come, signalling to locals that it's time to go fishing; westerly winds are stirring up the mullet and the snook are running too. Most days I see the fishermen cleaving the swell in their small boats, on their passage to a spot midway between Grassy and Middle Head where they will anchor. Up to twenty or so meet there to test their skills at tackle and baiting as they troll for a silver prize, bobbing in and out of the waves, their white and silver hulls glinting in the sunlight.

Our house is snug against the westerlies, and so sheltered on the mountain side that it's often too warm to wear a jumper outdoors. Even so, washing often takes the whole day to dry and, if I leave it until the sun's over Yarrahapinni, it's sometimes still slightly damp; I hold it to my face to feel if it's completely dry, as my tiny grandmother Foddy taught me, and breathe in the dewy freshness of it.

The tempo of autumn revitalises me. I wake gently with the sun and eventually rise to pick a pawpaw or orange for breakfast on the veranda with the dog at my feet. Bindi sleeps later these days and steps down rather tentatively from her trampoline bed. I suspect she might be suffering from a touch of arthritis but, if so, it never affects that happily wagging tail.

I write, I garden, I learn to set the fire. I cook recipes I've been saving for years, perfecting a wonderful date and walnut loaf (low fat), beer-battered local whiting (to impress visitors) and a Portuguese tuna empanada with golden yeast crust.

I read novels of murder and political conspiracy, and dally over the rural junk mail to unravel the arcane wealth of farm produce — calf cradles and broadcast spreaders, ATVs and head bails, unbeaked chickens and Dexter cattle. Fortunately for me, the pictures tell the story.

These days on my own are so pleasurable I feel almost guilty when I think of Christo working in Sydney, but he never complains and, when I see his headlights swing onto our road late on Wednesday nights, knowing he's been thundering along the highway with rock'n'roll blasting around him all the way, I feel a sense of excitement as if we've been apart for weeks.

Tonight I've baked the date loaf and its fruity fragrance blends with the pungent tang of wood smoke, seeping warmly through the house. As I watch Christo stride up from the garage, I think how handsome he looks in jeans and black leather jacket and take his icy face in my hands to kiss him. Bindi sits for a pat before she'll let him in the door.

'Brrrr ... let's get inside.' I can't wait to tell him my news. 'Something wonderful happened while you were away.'

'Oh yeah?' he chuckles. 'Can I put my bag down first?'

Flopping onto the chesterfield, I pick some fluff out of one of its buttoned pockets while he changes and comes back to join me. 'This young guy called Damon organised a meeting down at Michael and Irene's to see if we'd be interested in becoming part of a wildlife corridor, and I was invited.'

'Who's we?' he asks, crossing his feet on the coffee table, the one I call our 'good' coffee table even though it's fifteen years old and coming apart at the joins. Its legs sag sideways as Christo wriggles to find a comfortable possie.

'Careful ... your wine.' I make a grab to steady the wonky table. 'I didn't know the other people. They were from down the road. Jim was invited but couldn't make it.'

'So what's it all about?'

'Want a slice of date loaf?'

'Yeah, lovely.'

I cut it thickly, the way he likes it. But no butter. 'Well, apparently the government has grants for establishing wildlife corridors on private properties if the neighbours all agree. Damon has identified several sites, down as far as Taree I think he said, that would be suitable if he can get agreement from the landholders. Only four get the grants, and this area might be one of them if there's sufficient interest.'

Christo gets up to stir the fire. 'This is great cake, babe. I could smell it before I came into the house.' The flue control knob has had it, so he's improvised with a selection of stones he wedges underneath. 'What do we have to do?'

'Just agree to plant native trees on our land. Or we can have nesting boxes. But I'd rather have the trees.'

'I still don't understand. Is it a corridor that joins up with something?'

'Yeah, with the national park I think, so it's safe for native birds and animals to move around. I'm so excited about it — it's exactly what I've been wanting to do.'

'What will it cost us? Do we have to have it fenced off or anything like that?'

I'm a little short on actual detail. 'I think the idea is that the government grant covers the cost of the trees and all we need for planting them, and we provide the labour on a one-for-one dollar basis.'

'Hmmm ... sounds all right.'

'There's going to be another meeting and Damon will bring an aerial photo and tell us more.'

'Uh-huh. Where would we plant the trees?'

'I don't know but what I'd like to do, really like to do, is plant them at the dam.'

Christo laughs. 'You really do want to conduct weddings down there, don't you?'

'Don't mock me. It would be beautiful.'

We've already had a go at clearing away the head-high forest of weeds with the brushcutter and Christo's cane knife. It was slow progress, but we hacked a path (well, Christo did) through lantana and tobacco bush to the dam, where we discovered a large tree fern growing vigorously on the bank. Two smallish trees I couldn't identify, possibly natives, also grew at the water's edge. Finding these plants stirred my romantic soul — this is where we would begin our campaign for the environment.

That was the day Bindi became The Black Creature from the Lagoon, emerging from a futile attempt to catch three noisy ducks with her coat the colour and texture of tar, and stinking rotten. This muddy dip becomes a ritual. Whenever we go near the dam, she wades in just deep enough to coat her hide, frighten away the ducks and churn up the detritus that clings to her like treacle. She never seems to learn that paddling in the dam means a thorough hosing when we get home or, if she does, she's decided it's a small indignity to endure for the joy of every smelly second.

That night I dream of paperbark groves and banks of native orchids, a gravel path meandering to the dam, burrowing platypus, splashing water dragons ... and radiant brides.

Reading the shop windows at Stuarts Point is an irresistible local custom: the newsagency, the Four Square and Thommo the butcher on one side and the Point Café opposite display notices in their windows and, although they're often identical, we make sure we check them all. We don't want to miss anything important. A gearbox for sale. Tie-dyeing classes. The program for the Yarrahapinni Walking Group. Footy fundraisers. Some are written on neat slips of paper in a precise hand; others have been dashed off in marker pen. In two years, we've never missed doing the rounds.

So it's not surprising that, in our heightened state of environmental urgency, Christo and I respond to a notice in the newsagent's window inviting residents to join an organised walk along the river. The flier, headed up SPADCO (whatever that is), explains that the walk has been arranged to remind the community of the path's existence and to discuss its use and future enjoyment. To be followed by that foolproof crowd-pleaser, a sausage sizzle.

About thirty people turn up to the Community Hall on a morning that is absolutely perfect. Because we have Bindi with us, and also because we don't know anyone, we hang around on the fringes of the crowd.

'Hello, everyone,' calls a young woman surrounded by people who are obviously her mates. She's in serious bushwalking clobber, with lively smile and dancing eyes. 'My name is Nicky. Thank you all for coming. What a great turnout. I'd like to explain what we'll be doing today.'

We will walk along the track by the river, stop after a while to comment on what we've seen and volunteer ideas. It's an initiative of the Stuarts Point and District Community Organisation. Ah, SPADCO.

From the Community Hall it's impossible to see the entrance to the track because it's hidden by shrubbery and there's no marker, but two steps into the bush and there it is. Somewhat difficult to negotiate at first, the trail begins with a stumbling descent over a mangle of tree roots. Soon, however, it flattens out to a sandy path that wanders along beside mangroves and marshes, under weeping branches. Filtered light dapples the walk; it is damp in places, flushed by a tide now ebbing away.

Before long, 300 metres or so into the bush, Nicky gathers the walkers together and, as they toss ideas around and ask questions about insurance and signage and the environmental impact of its use, we learn that the path is mostly on land owned by the Seventh-Day Adventist Convention Centre. Apparently the SDA maintains the track and encourages the community to share it.

Bindi is becoming restless, so we slip away to complete the walk that twists away from the river at times through swamps and light forest. At one point, a timber landing juts out from the bush to hang over the quiet waters; from here we can see no one, no houses and (we count our blessings) no water-skiers. An osprey circles lazily, broad wings tilting into the thermal currents. Christo's sharp eyes have picked out a blue-tongue lizard clinging in disguise to a slim, mottled tree; a mullet flashes into sight briefly before flopping back into the water.

We complete the walk to discover that it finishes at Grassy Head. At the place we call home. My thoughts turn to the way Noosa and Byron Bay used to be, with simpler lifestyles and greed on hold. Change is inevitable, but this slow world Christo and I now inhabit is rare, unspoiled and it should stay that way.

We have joined the local licensed club. Not that we're club people; pubs are more our scene. Initially, we just went there for a look, strolling down the concrete path under the arched wrought-iron sign reading Stuarts Point Workers Club and past the bowling greens, the flagpole and dedication stone.

A smiling woman in uniform appeared as we walked in the door. 'Hello. How are you? Signing in, are we?'

Christo nodded.

'Um … sorry, sir, but you can't come in wearing a shirt without sleeves.'

Christo, in his Calvin jeans and smart new tank top, propped for a minute and was about to turn away.

'... but I'm sure we can find you something.' And in seconds she was back with a wink, a smile and a gaudy shirt. 'Looks great. My name's Jan. Now, what can I get you to drink?'

From time to time we went back until, on one occasion, we were discovered to be illegals; if you live within 5 kilometres of a club (as the crow flies), you are a certified local and must become members. That's when we joined. At $10 a year ($6 for seniors), why wouldn't we?

But we didn't become regulars until we had solved the Tuesday night mystery. On Tuesdays at around 5 pm, something compels a large number of the residents of Stuarts Point to leave their humble beach shacks, cream brick veneers and permanent caravans and hit the streets. Walking in pairs and groups or by themselves, riding motorised scooters that carry handbags and hats in neatly organised baskets and driving their cars, they flow into Ocean Parade to the seductive call of an unseen piper. Young and old, families and loners, they move as one into the club. By 5.30 pm, only a few stragglers remain on the street. Tuesday night is members' draw.

We can't take advantage of it, though, because Christo and the truck are in Sydney on Tuesday nights. Shame. We could use a cool $300.

Nights are getting quite chilly now, especially when the wind is up, and we're running out of firewood, having used all the off-cuts Brian left us. As a matter of fact, we're relieved about that because this is termite territory, which means not letting wood lie around. The destructive little ants love the stuff.

I've been looking in the local paper for firewood ads, without any luck. Maybe Greg will know someone. I stroll down the hill.

At first I'm not sure he's in the packing shed, even though I heard the ute cough into action this morning, because it's so dim inside; there's no power, and not much light is coming through the single sheet of corrugated fibreglass in the roof above the dipping bathtubs. But Greg's good ute is parked inside, its tray laden with cartons of bananas.

Dizzy comes rushing out to meet us from the back of the shed, which is when I spot Greg having lunch, feet up on a second chair as he reads the sports pages of his newspaper. I'm always hesitant to go into the packing shed; it's Greg's place. Bindi's the same, hanging around outside and sniffing at the old work boot while Dizzy keeps an eye on her.

'G'day, Greg. Sorry to interrupt your lunch.'

'You're right, I've just finished.' He manoeuvres a battered-looking lid into place on a battered-looking small cooler and pushes it to the far side of the table.

'Great lunch box,' I say to him.

'Used to be all right,' he replies, leaning back in his chair, arms folded behind his head. 'Before Bindi got at it.'

'Uh-oh. What happened?'

He starts laughing. 'Came back for lunch one day, lid was off, sandwich was all gone.'

'You're kidding? That's terrible.'

Greg shrugs. 'She left me the plastic bag, though. Now I keep my lunch box up on the table.'

I'll have to make him a cake, a banana cake.

Greg rises slowly from the chair, arching his back in a slow stretch. Nailed on the wall behind him is a roughly drawn map of our property, marked off in sections and numbered; the figure of a horse stands in the bottom right-hand corner near the dam, which is divided in half by a fence. Mark has told us a horse had died on the property years ago and been buried around there somewhere. Is that what Greg's horse drawing represents? I never get around to asking him.

'Well, I'd better get going. Here, Diz,' he says walking over to his ute; he places a perfect ripe banana on the floor in front of her and reaches back into the ute. 'Yeah, here's one for you, too, Bindi. No hard feelings.' Bindi looks at the proffered fruit with a puzzled expression, takes it in her mouth, then trots into the middle of the road to watch Dizzy.

'Ever seen this?' Greg says, nodding towards Dizzy.

The kelpie steadies the banana with one paw and uses her teeth to peel the skin back, then licks at the fruit with a dainty tongue until it's all gone.

Bindi and I are agog. What a smart little thing.

'So, what have you been up to lately?' Greg asks.

'Well, my herbs and chillies are going great guns. Had a few zucchinis. How's your place going?'

'Pretty good. Had some great avos this year. I've been meaning to come and see you. Things are going so well I should be out of your hair by the end of the year, I reckon.'

'Well, when you're ready. No hurry.' No hurry at all.

'I've already started giving some of the bananas the needle. Don't want to leave it all till the last minute.'

'It's a shame to kill 'em off after all your hard work, Greg. Oh, well ...' It does seem like a waste, but we're absolutely certain we don't want to farm bananas. Ever.

'Oh, by the way, the reason I came down ... Do you know anyone around here who sells firewood?'

'Firewood? There was a bloke up, um ... Why don't you just pick up some dry wood in the bush?'

Inwardly, I shake my head. Of course. There are plenty of trees on our land, and branches that have fallen on the ground.

'In fact,' he says, pointing, 'there's a bloody big log just behind you on the other side of the road.' Gulp. It's about the size of a telegraph pole.

'When Christo's back, tell him I'll give him a hand to get it up the hill. I've got a chain here somewhere. We'll hitch it up to your four-wheel drive.'

There has to be a point, I reassure myself, at which I finally become country-wise. It can't happen soon enough.

'Mama, it's me.' Alix, agitated. 'Our house is on fire. Well, it's not, but it was, and we can still smell smoke and we don't know what to do and we're really frightened and the fire brigade has been and we thought they fixed it but we can still smell smoke and the …'

'Hang on, slow down. Are you okay? What happened?'

'I just told you.' Slightly irritated. 'Can you put Dad on, please?'

I hand the phone to the Wise Parent and pace, anxious to know what she's saying as he nods and listens. 'Yep. Okay. I see. He did? Well, yes. I think so.'

Bloody hell, Christo. Hurry up. I motion him to pass me the phone but he ignores me.

'Yes, yes, you did the right thing. Call them tomorrow. Tell them what he said. Okay. Your mother wants a word. Okay.'

'Mama, I can't talk. Dad will explain everything. Hayley and I are going out to get something to eat.'

'Are you really all right?'

'Yes, Mama, honest. Don't worry.' Don't worry. She's been saying that since she was about a year old. I do try.

'Okay, darling. Talk to you later.'

While Christo puts me in the picture, I top up my wine. The girls had been cooking dinner when they smelled smoke, saw it pouring out of the kitchen cupboard containing the fuse box and called the fire brigade. The firefighters found that power to the stove wasn't earthed and had melted the fuse.

'We should never have left Sydney. Look at what's happened because of my selfishness.'

'Rubbish,' Christo retorts, a little sharply. 'The girls have done all the right things and they're going to show the melted fuse to the agent tomorrow so the wiring can be fixed. Look, it was pretty scary, but they handled it. I'm proud of them, especially Alix.'

'I guess you're right but … ' The tears have come, hot and heavy on my cheeks. 'I've always been worried it would all go wrong and now … '

He takes me in his arms. 'It's all over, darling, and Alix is fine. I'll take her to dinner when I'm in Sydney next week and make sure. Don't worry. Everything is all right.'

Totally out of the blue, Christo's been made redundant and is out of a job for the first time in his life. He rings me from a noisy mid-morning Sydney street, the frenetic sounds of city traffic interrupting his controlled delivery of the dreadful news. There are no details, just the facts, as he presents the information in a dispassionate monotone. He has to go back to work in a minute and I know he is trying to shield himself from emotional reaction and cushion the blow for me. What can I say to him, so far away on an anonymous city street? What can I do to ease the frustration and the anger? What rationalisation can I offer without dishing up platitudes? Nothing. Nevertheless, my mind darts around searching for some meaningful phrase or a darkly funny line. Instead, typically, I burble.

'Try not to worry. We'll be all right. I know we will.'

'I suppose so,' he replies. Although his voice is steady, I can hear the anguish.

'Well, it's probably not much consolation but at least I'll be much happier with you here all the time ... '

'Yeah, me too.'

'And you know how I hate you having to do that drive there and back every week ... I'm always scared you'll have an accident.'

'Yep.'

'We might even be better off financially, with the cost of petrol and wear-and-tear on the truck ...'

'Maybe.'

'And you will get some sort of pay-out, which will help ...'

'Yeah, babe, look, I gotta go. I'll call you tonight.'

He's to work for the next two weeks, he tells me later. There will be a severance package but, because he's not been with the company long, it won't be a big one. And because of the seven years we spent in New Zealand, where superannuation deductions are not compulsory, there won't be much joy there either.

It's not easy to stay positive, but it's in my nature to have a go so, when Christo arrives home for good late on that last day, there's a bottle of Rutherglen sparkling shiraz in the fridge and a well-rehearsed toast ready.

'To the next exciting chapter of our lives.' Clink. 'Darling, I've been thinking ... '

'Mmmm? Go on.' He's bracing himself.

'I think we should investigate selling Bondi Junction. I know we all love our little house, but ... '

'Hey, you don't have to talk me into it. I think it's the only thing we can do. But are you sure you want to?'

What alternative do we have? No regular income, two mortgages and half the rent on Alix's flat.

'Actually, I hate the idea. I think selling it could be a big mistake but I don't see another solution either, unless one of us finds a job up here.'

We agree to give it another few months. If one of us hasn't found work by then, we'll sell Bondi Junction. Job vacancies around here are rare, hard won and rarely surrendered. We pore over the positions vacant ads in the local paper, but neither of us has the experience or qualifications to be social workers, build roads, drive backhoes or manage timber yards. A background in the public service would help.

I apply for a part-time job compiling a newsletter for a Macksville school, something I'd love to do because it would involve me in the community; I meet all the requirements in the job description and should be a walk-up start, but I don't even make it to an interview. Surprised and not a little confused, I decide to go for a management role in Kempsey; I have years of management experience as a former editor, worked at the Queensland University of Technology as a guest tutor and full-time as a publishing manager, and I've sat around the odd boardroom table. But the pages and pages of selection criteria are daunting enough to stop a rabbit breeding! The application takes me two days to write and, once again, no interview.

The local paper doesn't want me and they don't want Christo either. He enrols in a bar course, even tops the class; but no experience, no job. He registers as a casual teacher, optimistic in this climate of too few male teachers; nothing doing. He even goes after an interesting (but low-paying) office position, gets an interview, gets a second interview but isn't told until three months later he didn't get the job.

Bloody hell. And now the stupid brushcutter won't start.

chapter ten

'To forget how to dig the earth
and to tend the soil
is to forget ourselves.'

Mahatma Gandhi

Things can't get much worse, I tell myself. Bills, rising petrol prices and mortgage interest payments that go up every time the Reserve Bank meets. The letting agent managing our terrace keeps emailing with problems in Bondi Junction that need our attention. Our tenants aren't happy with the TV reception; please fix. A tree branch has fallen into a neighbour's yard; please remove. Damp problems have shown up next door, thought to be coming from our place; please phone.

At least Alix is happy and doing well at uni this year, and we have Grassy. As a matter of fact, good things are starting to happen here. A bloke with a faint Kiwi accent phones about me doing some consulting work on a food magazine he's recently launched.

'It's called *recipes+*,' he says, introducing himself as Roger. 'Nothing but quick, easy affordable recipes for families on a budget, plus lots of tips and hints.'

Never heard of it, but I am all ears. Not just because I would like the work … I'm much more comfortable with a down-to-earth magazine than a glossy crammed with celebrity gossip.

Roger sounds young, excited, keen. 'We've had only three issues but it has heaps of potential, and I need someone with a good editorial background on board. From what I've heard, you would be perfect.'

I wonder if he knows I'm an old warhorse? Despite the PM's admonitions for people to work until they're seventy, it's difficult not to feel like an also-ran when you're surrounded by the cult of youthful omnipotence.

So I summarise my working life — which reveals my age with all the subtlety there can be when you've obviously been in the workforce for decades, to which point he replies with an engaging chuckle. 'I don't care how old you are, Gill, if you're the right person for the job.'

Roger wants to meet me, so I'm on the next plane to Sydney for the beginning of what turns out to be a terrific association. He's a lively thinker, a good listener, a true entrepreneur. I respond to his openness and warm to his passion during a long meeting laced with several cappuccinos. I miss good coffee.

He needs someone who can translate his magazine dream, he says, an old hand who knows talented people and the tricks of the trade. He needs me. Best of all, he's happy for me to work from home, and that's my ideal.

At about the same time, another stranger calls me — Sarah Wilson, editor of *Cosmopolitan* magazine. I've been recommended to fill a senior job vacancy until a full-time replacement can start. Me? On *Cosmo*?

For six weeks, I work with an amazing team of young women: intelligent, funny, hard-working and committed to making the world of their peers more informed and more enjoyable. *Cosmo's* 'we're-in-this-together' relationship with its twenty-something readers hooks me; it's a great magazine. I learn to wear lavender eye shadow to set off my green eyes, choose knee-length, wide-cut shorts to suit my body shape best and, well, much more that I no longer have any use for.

One of the feature writers strolls around to the sub-editors' area one day, saying, 'Hello, ladies. I need your help. Anyone of you have any funny stories about things that have happened to your vagina?'

Of course, we all look up immediately and break into laughter.

'I'm serious, guys.'

Am I embarrassed? Yep. Not by the topic, but because I can't think of a single funny thing that's happened to mine and I'd like to be part of the team.

Even so, they accept me — if not as one of them, then as a slightly eccentric visitor who's come onto their patch with skill and a sense of humour. And I'm very comfortable with that.

Our Sydney friends make it possible for me to work down there, putting me up — and putting up with me! I stay with the Bears, who actually seem to prefer having a full house to a quiet one; Barrie and Mary Ellen, who insists on preparing wonderful evening meals and freshly baked scones on Sunday mornings; and Rosie.

Rosie lives on the lower North Shore in a townhouse with its own private shady courtyard. Black-beaked pied currawongs call raucously to each other every morning from the leafy canopy of a giant elm outside the spare bedroom window, making me feel right at home. At night we watch telly, yarn and (often) drink a little too much red wine, and I'm reminded how lucky I am to have good friends.

As for Alix, she's so busy with uni and dance (studying and teaching) that I rarely catch up with her unless I tempt her to meet me for lunch or dinner. Being a student, of course, free food is irresistible and the bonus for me is the glow I feel when I'm with her. Christo and I wanted more children, but Alix was the only one of eight who made it past fourteen weeks.

'I'm glad I'm an only child,' she says, tucking into pasta with bolognese.

'Wait until Dad and I are old,' I warn her, mischievously. 'You'll have to push us around in wheelchairs all by yourself.'

'Ha. Don't worry. I'll put you both in a nursing home and only come to visit when it's my birthday.'

We joke, but it saddens me to think of her on her own. Christo and I talked of adopting but, being over thirty when we realised childbearing wasn't going to be easy for us, we didn't qualify. Briefly we toyed with the idea of an overseas adoption, expensive but possible, but finally we came to the opinion that children belonged in their own country. Who were we to say we could provide a better life?

An ectopic pregnancy — a trisomy, the worst of genetic abnormalities — when I was forty-one was our last attempt.

'It was a boy,' I told Christo, my heart aching as I stumbled through my tears from the doctor's surgery where I had learned the results of the laparoscopy.

But by then Alix was four and feisty, and a lovable handful. The pain faded eventually, as it had done before, and the Nicholsons remained a threesome.

Did we spoil her? Maybe. But I reckon there's not a lot wrong with raising a child with heaps of love. I like what I see in her as a young woman and we are very close, exchanging confidences, respect and dreams.

When we grab a bite together, we pack in all the news and gossip that's too complicated for texting. Not that I have anything very interesting to tell her; she says the country is a place you visit for two days at the most. Lovely, but …

She's bubbling over tonight, tells me she's performing at Dulwich Hill fair in two weeks, planning her twenty-first birthday, loving Psych, hating Statistics, enjoying Performance Studies and thinking about doing honours.

Alix will be the first graduate in the Nicholson family. Christo and I both quit uni in second year: he was more interested in folk music and left the New England University in Armidale for Brisbane; I was offered a journalism cadetship on the *Northern Territory News* in Darwin. The year was 1966.

Darwin was a blast of hot air as two teenage sisters stepped onto the shimmering tarmac. It was a town of late-night openers, where drinkers quaffed jugs of beer before they could get warm; weekend footy thrilling loud boozed-up crowds, the young Islanders and Aborigines making their mark with a spellbinding cross-pollination of their league and rules wizardry; glassy-eyed backpackers named Jock and Taffy and Mal banning party gatecrashers who came empty-handed; people going troppo in the relentless pressure of the Wet, hitting, screaming, killing; loners and outcasts; large Chinese families running the shops and market gardens; large

Greek families running the betting shops and fishing; too many men — men on the run from the law and their families, men working the mines down the track to blow it all on ponies and beer; drunken brawls outside the Aborigines' watering hole, the dirt-floor Don Hotel and paddy wagons waiting for their nightly catch; Aboriginal land rights, the Gurindji people and the landmark strike at Wave Hill station; Frank Hardy out-yakking Talking Tex Tyrell in the yarn-spinning competition at the Darwin Hotel; a legal system coming to terms (or, more often, not) with an ancient, confused, misunderstood culture.

For me it was all this, and the beginning of my journalism career, mentored by my editor Jim Bowditch — tiny, wiry, pugilistic, grizzle-haired, hard-drinking, ex-Z Force, defender of the underdog, the downtrodden, the Aborigines. Now long gone. I was eighteen.

```
SECRET
COMMONWEALTH OF AUSTRALIA
(A.S.I.O.)
                                    Brisbane.
                         29th February, 1968.
Deputy Director-General (N.S.W.) Operations
Regional Director, A.C.T.
Regional Director, Northern Territory
Copy to — Headquarters, A.S.I.O.


Gillian Fiona CHALMERS
In Northern Territory ██████████████     'Q'
Report No. 5/68 ████████████    dated 12th
January,   1968,   under   above   heading   (to
Headquarters,  New  South  Wales  and  Queensland
only)   it   was   mentioned   that   Gillian   Fiona
CHALMERS  had  been  recently  replaced  on  the
Northern Territory 'News' staff and would soon
```

leave Darwin for Sydney to take up a position on the staff of 'The Australian'.

2. Information has been received from ███████ ██████████ that Gillian Fiona CHALMERS is to take up a position with 'The Australian' in Canberra.

3. Gillian Fiona CHALMERS was born on 2nd May, 1947, Brisbane and she is a daughter of Hector Macdonald Chalmers (QPF 5098), the president of the Queensland Branch of the Australia — China Friendship Society, and Norma June CHALMERS (QPF 5555), Secretary of the Queensland Peace Committee for International Co-operation and Disarmament.

4. Whilst resident in Queensland Gillian Fiona CHALMERS was connected with the Queensland Youth Peace Committee, Queensland Peace Committee, Eureka Youth League, Youth Campaign Against Conscription and Society for Democratic Action. During her stay in Darwin she was relatively quiet, politically, however did identify herself with anti-Vietnam and peace demonstrations.

5. It would be appreciated if addressees could make enquiries to establish the current whereabouts of Gillian Fiona CHALMERS.

███████████████████

Regional Director,Queensland

From documents obtained from the Australian Intelligence Association under the Freedom of Information Act.

What a threat I was, with my dangerous notions of world peace, international cooperation and understanding. It's just as well ASIO tapped my phone and watched me from unmarked cars. Who knows what I might have done after demonstrating against war and singing about the brotherhood of man? I might even have become a greenie …

Damon rings the day after I get home from Sydney to tell us the grant has come through. We're going to plant our rainforest at the dam. However, we need to complete the forms itemising the project's costs and identifying our contribution; he's on his way up so we can sign them.

'Big swell today,' Damon says, hanging over the veranda rail with us. 'Might go for a surf later.' It's one of those extremely rough days, waves jetting so high into the air they're almost level with the top of Grassy.

'Looks a bit wild to me,' I reply.

'Yeah,' Damon agrees, grinning, before dragging himself away from the view to get out the papers he's brought. He mutters to himself and starts writing.

'You'll need mulch for two hundred and fifty trees, about forty bales, some Roundup Biactive, red marker dye, pig wire.'

I interrupt swiftly. 'Hang on, did you say two hundred and fifty trees?' Sounds like a helluva lot to me.

'Yeah, two hundred and fifty won't go far,' he smiles. 'Ah, will you be using pig fencing or tree guards?'

Christo answers. 'Ummm, well, what ... '

'Never mind. It's about the same cost. Plus the tube stock. I reckon that will balance out against your labour.'

We trust his enthusiasm implicitly.

'Where do we get the trees?' Christo asks.

'A place up past the Pub With No Beer called Thumb Creek Nursery. Do you know it?'

Blank looks. 'We know where the Pub With No Beer is,' Christo says. 'I'm sure we could find it.'

'You might not have to,' Damon replies. 'I think they have an arrangement where they leave big orders in Macksville. But I'd talk to Margaret and Jim. They're going to plant on the other side of the road, and it might be an idea to liaise with them about the type of trees that are suitable for this area.'

Better still, let's order the same trees. I like the symbolism of neighbourly forests.

'I'll get these forms off today ... maybe after I've been for a swim,' Damon says, grinning again. 'Just one thing. The project has to be completed by the end of January, so allow yourselves enough time to clear and fence the land, spray circles for the tube stock and get your stakes in. You said you'd supply the stakes, didn't you?'

Christo nods. He attended a follow-up meeting while I was in Sydney.

Damon's off to Margaret and Jim's. 'Any questions, give me a ring. Catch you later.'

Questions? Clear and fence the land? Spray circles? With what, and why? I hope Christo knows what it all means. It's November already.

'Er ... darling?' I'm not sure I should ask this question. 'Have you ever built a fence?'

As our wedding anniversary approaches along with another 'reminder' from the ATO about my Pay-As-You-Go arrears, our finances aren't looking as rosy as we'd like, but the work in Sydney has triggered my happiness switch and I talk Christo into celebrating this year at a BYO Italian place we've heard of in Macksville.

'What street's it on?' Christo asks as we drive under the Warrell Creek overpass to join the highway south of Macksville.

'Don't know what it's called, but the restaurant is on the corner of the street leading up to the TAFE. Do you know where the TAFE is, love?'

'No.'

'Turn left at the lights at Macksville RSL, then right, go down past Dangerous Dan's and the Short Order Café, turn left and Giardino's is down that street.' I should have checked the name of it when I booked, but I'm pretty sure this is the right street.

Nothing stirs as we drive along, past a coach-building yard locked up behind a 10-metre high wire fence and old timber cottages reinvented as offices for a surveyor and a beautician.

'Oops. There … go back,' I call, and he pulls over. Without daylight saving, we would have missed it.

'Back there, on the corner, see the house with a light out the front?'

A faded sign lit by a single beam stands on the lawn of faded house that was once painted deep apricot. 'Giardino's Garden Restaurant', says the sign, but we still can't see the restaurant itself. Just the house.

Then I spot it. 'Look … around the corner.' Christo executes a three-point turn to bring us up behind a handful of cars.

Up a driveway at the back of the house, two lattice-covered doors are propped open to reveal a romantic courtyard: lush greenery spills over trellised walls surrounding candlelit tables clothed in red-and-white check. It's perfect.

Robust smells waft from the kitchen, Italian music oozes from somewhere inside and there's something else, an aroma I notice the minute we enter. I sense, inhale something familiar but unexpected as we are seated … yes, that's it. Under our table, and all the others, immersing diners in a smoky protective haze, is a mozzie coil.

We have a lovely night, putting away our cares and simply enjoying being together. The rustic Italian menu includes one of my old favourites, veal cooked in marsala, and the dish sends me into raptures. Christo goes for a pizza. A wonderful meal, and all up it is less than $60.

Christo raises his glass of red from the bottle we brought (an indulgence; we are penny-pinching cask wine drinkers these days). 'Thank you for a wonderful life, babe. Things might be falling apart around us, but I don't regret a minute of our life together.'

We clink glasses. 'Me, too. We are very, very lucky to have each other.'

'You know, Christo, I've been thinking. Why don't we restate our vows again next year? We've been talking about doing it for so long ... and next year is our twenty-fifth.'

On Christmas Day 1996 in New Zealand, under the rose-covered arbour in the garden of our friends the Parkinsons, I had asked Christo to 'marry' me again. I admit I was in my cups, but so what? Our wedding day had been so wonderful. Why not reaffirm our vows with old friends and new and throw a big party?

'Okay, you're on. But we'll have to start planning now.'

For a minute or two there's a silence between us. I'm remembering our wedding day in the garden at Lane Cove as the sun set over the river, fifty hand-picked guests (all we could afford — nothing much has changed there), how I fluffed my vows and got the giggles, the gifts that have survived (one crystal goblet and a beaten copper jug), friends no longer 'with us' and our joyful promise to each other then never to give up wearing jeans ...

The next day, we formally make the decision we knew we would have to, to sell Bondi Junction, and reluctantly begin the process of parting with our little terrace as soon as possible. But the market seems to have gone a bit flaky. Wait until after Christmas, the agent advises, no one buys over Christmas. The disgruntled tenants move out. For the six weeks until auction there will be no rental income.

The stress is almost unbearable. Will we sell? Will we get a good price? Will our finances hold out until then? I'm splitting my time between Grassy and Sydney, where I'm tarting the house up for inspection — washing walls, gardening, replacing carpet, fixing dripping taps.

Rosie offers to come to Bondi Junction one weekend to help me paint skirting boards and architraves, though I get to do the architraves because she doesn't like being up on ladders. Fair enough.

Even with her help, the tension generated by deadlines and anticipation has become so bad I have to concentrate on not hyperventilating as I work. Up and down the ladder, move the ladder along, fill the brush with paint, don't dribble it on the floor, up again and … I'm almost finished the bedroom. Dizzily, I climb down from the ladder, calf muscles wobbling in protest at the unaccustomed step workout and, in a dream, watch myself plant one foot into the roller tray full of paint. The colour? Bottle green. Gloss enamel.

'Rosie, help,' I cry, lifting my dripping foot as the paint soaks through from the runner into my sock. My foot feels warm and gluggy.

She rushes out of the bedroom and is back in seconds, not with a rag, not with a towel — with a camera.

'No … it's not funny,' I plead. 'Don't do this to me. Help me.'

All she can do is laugh and I'm laughing, crying with her.

'Now will you get me a rag? Please.'

'All right. But I want you to stop for the day. Clean up and we'll go and get something to eat. It'll all be over soon, Gilly.'

And then it's back to Grassy. On a beautiful, cloudless afternoon a week before Christmas I fly into Coffs Harbour,

Christo waiting there in the crowd with boyish smiles and a bear hug. Everything is all right again. A crescent moon floats over Grassy as we climb the drive; a family of three wallabies interrupts their grazing to eye us suspiciously. Bindi greets us at the garage with leaps of love.

'I've missed you so much,' I tell Christo, taking his free hand as he grabs my travel bag from the car.

'Me, too. You're lovely.'

My hand instinctively goes to my hair, ratty and streaked with the yellow paint I used on the bedroom walls. 'I look terrible,' I retort.

'Never. What's a bit of yellow paint?' He strokes my head lovingly, tucking a strand of my flyaway hair behind one ear. 'Now. Would you like a beer? I'm going to have one. Glass of wine, perhaps?'

We sit outside, inhale the evening, swap news.

'Bloke's coming tomorrow to clear around the dam,' Christo tells me.

At last, the rainforest project is starting.

By 10 am, the dozer has knocked down the lantana, bracken and tobacco bush, piling it into the centre so we can burn it off. I can't believe we (we?) ever thought we could clear it with a brushcutter and cane knife.

Exposed now, the dam looks stunning. Water lilies cover half the surface with their huge leaves and we can see right to the other side where wattles cling tenuously to the swampy soil. Remnants of an old barbed wire fence disappear into the middle of the dam, one sagging timber fence post poking up through the water lilies, then re-emerge on the neighbouring property.

With the whole area flattened we discover a creek — small, but still a creek — struggling into the dam through a tangle of fallen branches, weeds and fallen logs. The sluggish flow is a sludgy rust colour.

A secret creek, my head says. We can bring it to life. Water will run again, sluicing it clean; wildlife will come, frogs and water dragons; birds will drink, and drop seeds from our native trees. Simple. Real. Connection. I am high on possibilities.

We have a permit to burn the hill of rubbish the dozer left behind and, relieved after our previous experience that the pile is quite sodden following the first real downpour of summer, set it alight.

It takes three days for the heap to burn down to a mound of smoky hot ash. The next step is to poison the weeds, but that can wait until after Christmas.

Already the mood of holiday celebration is in the air as the caravan park once more becomes a village. Fairy lights drip gaily from tents, brightly coloured cloths transform card tables and trestles, towels hang festively from rope lines and friendships flourish late into the night. Someone strums a guitar.

Sun-pink kids laugh and squeal and wrestle as night falls, sausages and onions sizzle greasily, fishermen tend to rod and reel, a group of Middle Eastern campers prepares a feast of spicy delicacies, fathers pull on beers, mothers sip from a cask going soggy in the Esky, surfers talk of breaks and swell … In a few weeks they will depart, leaving behind patches of tent-browned grass and a lingering resonance that's trodden into grains of sand by running feet, sparkling in the webs of mosquito-fat spiders, wriggling under the rope-etched bark of the banksias and mirrored in the eyes of goannas who see all.

chapter eleven

'"Now, teach me, little blue wren," said he.
"'Tis you can unravel this riddle for me.
I am 'mazed by the gifts of this kindly earth —
Which of them has the greatest worth?"
He flirted his tail as he answered then,
He bobbed and bowed to his coy little hen.
"Why, sunlight and worms!" said the little blue wren.'

CJ Dennis, 'The Growth of Sym'
from *The Glugs of Gosh*, 1918

Menacing coal black clouds have been accumulating all day over South West Rocks, now bathed in a surreal grey-green light. A strident wind lashes the sea into curling waves and thrashes Margaret and Jim's trees into a frenzy, flaying their strong slender trunks with unrelenting force. Eagerly we await the storm, the first of summer; Grassy Head isn't the Great Sandy Desert, but the mid-north coast is getting desperate for rain. By late afternoon rain-swollen cloud is all around us, one mass sweeping across the horizon and another looming behind us over Yarrahapinni, yet directly above us, patches of blue defy the cumulonimbus mass.

It's not until mid-evening that the storm finally breaks with flashes of sheet lightning, rolling thunder and, finally, the rain. The wind, far from abating, has strengthened, whistling and whipping the rain before it, driving it across the veranda with such momentum we have to struggle to close the sliding glass doors. We hear the precious rain striking the chimney in staccato bursts as loud as hail, and gurgling along the parched gutters to the tank. Thank heavens.

'Uh-oh. Did the lights just flicker or was it my imagination?'

'No, it's a brownout,' Christo says. It's the term we picked up from our graphic designer friend Sharon, who did her city-to-the-bush thing years ago when she moved to the Byron Bay hinterland. Shaz is well versed in power problems of the country kind. A brownout is a dip in power, often forewarning of a blackout, and a sure sign to unplug the computer.

'Might be nothing,' he replies.

So far the telly is still giving us a picture, although electronic disturbances sizzle across the screen occasionally. Thunder crashes so loudly the house shakes.

'Damn. There they go again.' Christo gets up from the chesterfield, but we're in darkness before he gets to the candles and matches in the kitchen.

'Power's gone,' he says unnecessarily, fingers fumbling along the ledge where we keep our emergency supplies. We're getting country-wise too.

As he strikes a light, I go to call Country Energy and then remember it's dangerous to use the phone in an electrical storm. What the heck. I know what they'll say. 'There have been disruptions to the power supply in the following areas [blah, blah] and power will be restored as soon as possible.' In other words, there's no point whingeing; they'll get to us when they can.

So we move outside with wine and mozzie coils and find the wind has dropped suddenly, as if someone turned off the power switch. Might as well sit and watch the show.

The rain has settled into a steady, heartening downpour. Silhouetted against the dazzling display of lightning, the spiky fronds of the cycads that Brian bequeathed to us and I planted in front of the veranda, dip and dance in the water fall.

Bindi loves the commotion. Ears stiffly alert and tail at the ready (for what, I can't imagine), she stands poised and purposeful. Christo calls her to his side and she affectionately leans her full weight on his thigh as he rubs her ears. He moves Bindi's bedding to the far side of the veranda where it's dry, and she follows him to see what he's up to: ever curious. She will always be a puppy.

The storm drifts north, we yarn about our past and our future, the candle flame flickers, the wine runs out, all is calm. Time for bed. We fall asleep to the thunder's distant boom and the trickling music of the rain.

Some time around midnight, the clock radio startles us awake with an urgent buzzing and frantic flashing lights. Christo slaps it and, when that doesn't work, snatches the radio up to set the time and give us peace. 'Now if we had a generator, this wouldn't happen.'

I roll away, mumbling 'uh-huh' into my pillow and smiling to myself because the radio is on his side of the bed.

By the time we wake up next morning, the cloud mass has moved on.

'Have you noticed you can see the Christmas bush from here now?' I ask Christo as we breakfast on the veranda. Although they're not in flower any more, the pale green of new growth is plainly visible past the bedraggled bananas. 'Look there, and down there.'

As the poisoned bananas die back, we're able to see more of our property: the sprawling old mulberry tree on the main track down to the pump has come out of hiding and is no doubt now alive with the tiny native bees that draw on its sweetness before the birds arrive; the avenue of mangoes running down the hill from the chook house, bare of fruit as they have been every year since we arrived, is now in full view; and, way over the back in the national park, a stark, white, leafless tree stands out like dog's balls. Maybe an osprey pair is nesting there.

'Greg isn't interested in Christmas bush anymore. You know, maybe Mary Ellen and Kerrie and Rosie are all right and we should be cutting it and selling it in Sydney.' I realise that I no longer consider myself city-smart; our friends in Sydney know better.

Christo's eyebrow arches, the one that indicates he's listening. 'Well, I suppose we could.'

'Why don't we at least look into it and see what's involved?'

'Sure, babe. If you want to.'

We really have to get serious about making an income from the farm. Apart from anything else, when the bananas are all gone it will become a full-time job just to keep it cleared — not a very practical or profitable use of the land.

It's sad to see the bananas go. They've been grown on our slopes for almost one hundred years and, for much of that time, those harvested on our northern slope were considered the finest in the district. But even if you know what you're doing with bananas, it's tough to make a living from them. Queensland is where the banana money is; its farms supply 95 per cent of the nation's total. Our bananas on the mid-north coast might taste better because they mature more slowly, but the fast returns are up north.

We'll keep a few bananas at the bottom of our orchard; I can't bear to part with them altogether. I miss their shivery sighs right outside our bedroom window, the curtain of green surrounding the house, the sound of Greg's knife whacking the bunches free and Dizzy yapping the old ute into life. Greg's farming only those bananas farthest from the house these days, the most productive, and he's rarely here.

I begin my Christmas bush research with a call to the Department of Ag in Coffs, our nearest office.

'Shame,' he says. 'You just missed a really big conference we held in Kempsey on cut flowers. Look, if you want to tell me where you live I could pop in next time I'm down your way.'

That's not soon enough. I want to get going now.

Our friends the Wilsons, who run the Yarrahapinni Homestead B&B, have a neighbour who can help. David and his son-in-law Alec grow cut flowers and it takes just one phone call to organise the pair to come and inspect our trees. These two generous strangers tramp with us through the chest-high African grass, tripping over rocks and potholes, to reach the plantation and give us their advice. Alec's been at this for ten years; now David, recently retired, has caught the bug and is experimenting with growing flannel flowers and Hinchinbrook banksia.

Over the next hour or so, the two enthusiasts demonstrate how to prune the straggly shrubs and explain irrigation techniques, fertiliser requirements and the relative merits of using weed mat. They absolutely refuse any payment for their time; success in this business is about sharing ideas and information, they say. Besides, they're setting up a co-op and hope to encourage more landholders to establish cut flower crops.

'Christmas bush is a lot of intensive work,' Alec warns, although his matter-of-fact tone suggests that he doesn't mind the labour. 'But it all happens over about six weeks of the year, so that's not so bad.'

Sounds good to me, and I notice Christo's listening attentively.

Overseas markets are the best, David says, because the Christmas bush harvest around here occurs too early for Sydney. 'The Japanese like the long symmetrical stems; the Americans like bunches. So there's very little wastage.

'But you won't make a fortune. Prices aren't as good as they were a few years ago,' he adds, his knife-sharp secateurs snipping at a wispy branch trailing on the ground. 'I'd say, looking at your set-up, you could possibly gross about $10,000 a year.'

Ten thousand. Well, that's something.

'But you won't get a good harvest this year. You should have already done your pruning.'

Our first harvest would be, let's see, about twenty-two months from now. Damn. Looks like it's time to find more work in Sydney.

It's been raining for three days. 'Got some healthy looking puddles out there,' Christo reports from the bedroom window. He's always first up, checking the day. 'Coffee?'

'Lovely. Thank you. Can I have a cappuccino?' Alix gave us an espresso machine for Christmas. Now Christo is a barista.

While he's grinding the beans, I put on a wash. I'm going to launder absolutely everything that's even slightly grubby now there's plenty of water, and hopefully there'll be more rain tonight. It certainly feels humid enough for another downpour.

'What time do we have to be down at the dam to meet the neighbours?'

'I don't think we made a time. We just said we'd see them there.' It's almost 10 am.

I help Christo load the truck. One 100-metre roll of hinged-joint standard galvanised pig wire, one roll of 4 millimetre gal wire for attaching pig wire to stakes, metal irrigation pipes, tool box, sledge hammer, mattock, spade, gloves and a few sharpened wooden stakes.

We're catching up with Margaret and Jim's Adelaide branch of the family, who are up here to plant their side of the private road. Their daughter Wendy and her husband Chris are already hard at it when we pull up beside our impressive pile of mulch — forty bales is a mountain of hay.

Their younger boy Michael, a tall, lean, gregarious fourteen-year-old, is holding a ladder, his father at the top hammering in a wooden stake.

'So, is your fence going up today?' Chris calls out, giving us a wave that sends the ladder tipping dangerously.

'Hold it steady, Michael.' Wendy appears from behind a Sally wattle, a small tree in one hand. They've planted hundreds of trees on Margaret and Jim's place, coming up from Adelaide a couple of times a year during the school holidays, and they're old hands at this.

Their wallaby fortifications are finished, pig wire stretched firmly between old banana stakes and the fence anchored at the bottom with irrigation pipes and more stakes. Wallabies go under fences, they tell us, not over them — that's kangaroos.

'Well, we'll at least make a start,' Christo replies. He's pieced together the basics of what's involved after talking to Damon and Jim, and we can use our neighbours' fence as a template for ours. Now we just have to put it all into practice.

It's a stinking hot day, distant rumbles warning us that there are more storms to come. I'm glad of the safari hat protecting my face, but the sun is a real scorcher even at this hour and it occurs to me that the tiny air holes in my hat might mean I end up with spotty sunburn.

'We'll start at the big wattle up near the road and use it as a straining post,' Christo says.

A quizzical glance from me.

'You need strong corner posts to help keep the fence taut,' he explains. 'Then we'll go down towards the dam to those two wattles close together and turn again. Then along the dam to that old fence post on the water's edge, up in front of the mango tree and around an old straining post that's there already. Then back to the first wattle.'

Sounds like a good plan to me.

Because of last night's storm most of the ground is soft, making it easy to get to all the perimeter stakes in by lunchtime.

Our neighbours, sensibly, are quitting for the day but we decide, anticipating shade and a cool afternoon breeze, to return to the dam to begin fencing.

Unrolling pig wire is possibly an acquired skill. The roll is extremely heavy, tightly wound and resists manipulation with the steely resolve of a Mallee bull, either springing back to its preformed shape when we try to unravel it or escaping down the creek bank until it is tangled in lantana. The cut ends thwart us too, catching on the parent roll time after time and refusing to let go.

But despite cut hands and bruised thighs, erecting the first side is easier than we expected. Christo wants to get all the pig wire in place today, then come back to weigh it down with the pipe tomorrow.

The heat is really getting to me. Although my job is simple, to cut lengths of gal wire and tie the fencing to the stakes, sweat runs down my nose constantly, steaming up my glasses, which occasionally slide right off my nose to the ground. The sweatband inside my safari hat is sodden. Surely it will rain soon.

'Honey, why don't we stop soon and go for a swim.' I envy Bindi. Black with mud and dripping wet, she squirms and stretches out in the shade of a small grove of tree ferns.

Christo is red in the face. I want him to stop and rest, but no such luck. 'Can you hang on for a bit longer? I'd like to turn the corner around those two wattles.' There's about 1 metre between them. 'That's where I'm going to make a bit of a gate.' I guess that will be for my benefit; he has no trouble straddling the fence.

At 5 pm, we pack up. It's nowhere near sunset, but the sky is gloomy with cloud coming in from the south-east, a repeat of yesterday. Rain or no rain, I'm going swimming. Now.

The next day we have the sense to start early, but the South Australians still beat us to it. 'Fence is coming along well,' Chris observes encouragingly, strolling across to our barren piece of soon-to-be-lush rainforest. He gives the pig wire a practised tug, nodding approvingly at Christo. 'Nice and tight. I see you used the wattle as a straining post. Good idea.'

To me he says, apparently noticing my runners for the first time, 'You're the one who's been doing the spraying then?' They are splotched bright pink from the red dye we mixed into the weedicide. I made quite a colour statement while spraying down the cobbler's pegs, clover and tall grasses that erupted after we'd finished the clearing ... spotty pink hands and legs, jaunty green-and-gold backpack. Thankfully my skin has faded to a lightly sunburned look now, but my runners!

Glyphosate is supposed to break down in the soil, and the type we're using is frog-friendly, but I wouldn't want to drink the stuff.

When we came here, I was determined we wouldn't ever use pesticide or weedicide, even if that meant tackling the whole property Rosie-style, plucking weeds by hand. Today I'm more relaxed about it (although I have a problem with some of the pest preparations: they kill bees) and, believing that poisoning the weeds here is a means to a good end, even feel a sense of pride in the arid landscape I've created. All that remains inside the bit we're fencing off is a big old wattle.

I hold open my palm to show him my red fingertips. 'Yep, I'm the weedkiller in the family.'

'How many times did you have to spray it?'

'Twice.' Soil wasn't meant to be bare. Two weeks after applying the poison, the weeds were back. 'That seemed to do the job.'

He looks around slowly, nods. 'Hmmm. Very thorough. That'll get the trees off to a great start. By the way, I've brought over our parrot's-head pliers. We've finished with them and thought you might find them useful to get the fence good and taut.'

He walks to the first stake along the fence line and, with a series of grab-and-twist movements, tightens the gal wire, taking up the slack in the fence.

'It's quite nifty,' he says, handing me the pliers. 'Actually, the boys have the knack. They could probably show you better than me.' He and Wendy, a dead-ringer for her mother, have two teenagers, David and Michael, and Anna, who's just started school.

'Look, I won't hold you up. Let us know if there's anything we can help you with.'

During the next couple of days we ask and learn many things. Wendy and Chris, working with Margaret and Jim, have reclaimed several hectares of land, some planted with cabinet timbers, some with rainforest specimens.

Our next job is to anchor the fence at the base, a slow and tedious task that involves hefting the heavy metal piping into place, passing some gal wire through and attaching it to the fence. I work the parrot's-head pliers to tension the fence; Christo bends to the task of making it impenetrable at the bottom.

And when that's done, we're still not ready for planting. First we have to drive in the stakes — two hundred and fifty of them, one for each tree. Over the past few weeks, we've been gathering up spare banana props, measuring them at 1.5 metres, sawing them to length and adding a sharp point. The stakes aren't to support the trees, they're to mark the spots where they'll be planted, roughly 2 metres apart.

'When you plant them close together, they compete for space and light and that makes them grow faster,' young Michael tells us. He's come to lend a hand, much appreciated for his knowledge as well as his strength and enthusiasm.

Christo and Michael whack in the stakes using the sledgehammer, and I have a go too, but ten is about my limit. I can hardly hold it above the stakes, let alone thump them. (There is a much easier method for embedding stakes in the ground, and that is to use a tool called a post driver. A post driver is a slim but heavy steel sheath; you lift it over the stake or picket using two long handles at the side and then drop it with force, which is pretty easy since it's so heavy. All you need essentially is the strength to position it over the stake. We learn about this tool several months after we've finished planting – from my sister Janet, who has one!)

So while that's going on, I calculate where to position each stake, measuring the distance between them in two long strides – which would be fine, except that the ground has a few bumps and hollows and my stepped-out placements are a trifle rough and ready. We're about halfway through placing the stakes when we realise that our grid pattern has straggled from Melbourne CBD precision to downtown Sydney maze.

It won't matter, will it? Too late now.

At the end of the day, another stinker, Christo and I stand back and admire our preparations. His unshaven face is crusted with dust, legs spattered with lumps of the blue clay we encountered somewhere in the middle.

'I don't think I've ever worked so hard physically,' I say to him. 'Except for the times we moved house. Are you enjoying it, love?'

I know how he will answer, but want to hear it, to be reassured that this dream of mine is working for him too. 'Yes.' Pause. 'Yes, I am.'

Taking off his hat, Christo wipes the dirty sleeve of his T-shirt across his even grimier forehead. Being made redundant really flattened him, but now Christo is more relaxed than I've ever known him. His stroke was brought on by work stress and I will never let that happen to him again.

'How about we wash away the dirt with a swim and then have a beer?'

'Sounds good to me,' Christo says. 'But first, a hug.'

As he holds me close, Bindi joins us from her swampy retreat and sits at our feet; she wants a hug, too. No way. A pat on the head will have to do.

After five days working in stifling heat and oppressive humidity, we're exhausted; our legs and backs ache from bending and lifting. Mozzies have managed to find secret ways through our clothing to bite our flesh, and at night our sleep is fractured by relentless itching. Bindi's coat is starch-crisp with putrid muck. Just as well we're having fun.

Today, the planting fun starts. There they are under one of the wattles, those two hundred and fifty plants in black plastic tubes crammed into four polystyrene crates from the Thumb Creek Nursery. Our neighbours did the ordering: some are fast growing and will provide protection for the understorey plants, some are more shrub than tree, some are havens for wildlife. All are listed by name on a typed sheet (botanical and common names); each has a green identification tag. How can we go wrong?

The plants are so small I recognise only a few of them: cycads I know, and bangalow palms and native ginger.

'Here are a couple of your fast growers,' Chris points out, giving their scientific names.

Michael leans over the selection, adding, 'Ooh, you've got kodas. I love kodas.'

'Paperbark,' Chris adds, turning to another crate. 'And here's your bleeding heart, a good pioneer plant. Do you have a plan for where you'll plant things?'

'It would be nice to have a palm grove near the dam, maybe with some ginger,' I say tentatively. 'But as for the rest, we haven't got a clue. I'd love you to make some recommendations.'

And so we begin. Chris advising, Christo digging the holes wide and deep to loosen the soil, me planting, and Michael applying himself energetically to any part of the process that flags.

The first row is at the edge of the drive. I'm overawed by the grand-sounding names written on the little green labels: *Flindersia schottiana* (silver ash), *Elaeocarpus grandis* (blue quandong), *Syzygium francisii*, *S. oleosum* and *S. australe* (lilly pillies), *Rhodomyrtus psidioides* (native guava), *Leptospermum brachyandrum* and *L. petersonii* (lemon-scented ti-tree), *Duboisia* (corkwood).

They're a mystery to us now, but one day, one day … the silver ash will thrust its broad trunk to breathtaking heights, the berry-laden quandong will bring birds to spread its willing seed and we will make jams from the tart fruits of *Syzygium australe* and the native guava, inhale the musty, papery bark of the *L. brachyandrum*, rub the pungent ti-tree leaves onto our arms to repel mosquitoes, Aborigine-style, and doze in the shade under the dense cover of the *Duboisia*.

How many rainforest specimens can you plant in a day? We manage just ninety-eight, patting a lemon-scented ti-tree firmly into the damp, fragrant soil near the dam just as the afternoon is wearing out. Me, too. And I reckon Christo will go a beer when we get back home. But there's still more work to be done. Every plant needs to be watered.

Here's where the neighbours' system with the stakes comes in. Not only do they mark the position of the small trees so you can avoid spraying them when you're dealing with weeds later, but also it's a guide to the next crucial step: watering.

After a tree is planted, you place its container upside-down on the stake; this indicates it still must be watered. When it's been watered, you remove the pot and next time you're in Macksville, you do the responsible thing – return the lot of them to Thumb Creek Nursery.

Wendy and Chris recommend a bucket of water for each plant, and it must be done the day it's planted. This'll be interesting. The nearest tap is 700 metres away, underneath the packing shed.

'How are we going to water the plants, love?' Christo asks. He thinks I have a plan and I do, of sorts.

Flourishing two buckets, I squelch into the slime at the dam's edge, Bindi joining in delightedly. I dip, fill and lumber up the slope.

'Now I'll hand this bucket to you over the fence and when you come back I'll give you the second full one and refill the first.'

'Righto.' Patiently, he stays with the plan for about eight of the plants.

'Hang on,' he says, depositing the buckets at my feet and marching back to the truck. He returns with a long yellow nylon rope, ties it to the bucket handle and tosses it into the dam. 'I think this will work better.'

It's not easy to keep a bucket upright, and full, when it's being dragged through bulrushes and over uneven ground but Christo persists. Sixteen plants watered, eighty-two to go. Today. Before we can stop.

'I reckon my way is faster,' I grin, grabbing the other bucket. 'I'll race you. Whoa … ' And slip down the slope straight into the dam. Feet lost somewhere in the ooze, thighs grazed from the rough ride over bracken, there is nothing to do but laugh and make the last decision of the day. We'll plant and water again tomorrow and the next day we should be finished.

And then we'll mulch each one. And then we'll water them all again. And then we'll come back and spray a new flush of summer weeds. And then we'll spray a new flush of autumn weeds. And then, and then …

'After a couple of years,' Damon assures us later when he comes to approve our efforts for his records, 'the canopy will have closed and you won't have to worry about weeds any more.' Smiling widely, he presents us with a weatherproof sign attributing the source of the grant. We're to hang it on the fence.

'You've done a great job. I'll be bringing around some government blokes to see what you and Jim and Margaret have done. Congratulations.'

I'm thrilled to bits. Even more excited than the day I set up the winning goal for our girls' soccer team in the 1964 grand final. We have planted a rainforest.

Our lovely little terrace has been on the market for three weeks and dozens of people have traipsed through. We've decided not to go down to Sydney for the auction but, when the day arrives, we're just as nervous as if we were there.

Christo collects the newspaper from the letterbox while coffee is brewing. Taking the paper out of the plastic bag, he tosses it onto the dining table. 'Sydney house prices plummet' screams the front-page headline. It might as well read, 'Nicholsons, you're buggered'. We don't receive one bid.

chapter twelve

'Happiness is not a goal but a
consequence, a result of how we live
our lives; it's not found by focusing
narrowly on our own personal desires
but by bringing others into the equation
of our concerns and goals.'

Richard Eckersley, National Centre for Epidemiology
and Population Health at the 2004 Communities in Control conference

Things are bustling next door. Mark has a new wife, Brenna, a sparky Californian photographer with enough energy to set the woods on fire, which she virtually does. Apparently unfazed by the isolation of our shared hilltop, she gets cracking, terracing around their house with rocks, planting sweet peas and eggplant, and sewing curtains. Brenna always has her camera ready to capture the moment, fascinated by her new world.

Before long, while we're playing at being mini-environmentalists down at the dam, Mark teases his stubborn tractor into action and the newlyweds plant a cash crop of zucchini and squash on the far hillside, as well as some Christmas bush and kangaroo paw.

We rarely see them, although we often hear Brenna's sweet, serious-minded nine-year-old daughter Perryn and Mark's two youngsters, Andee and Jas, squealing and splashing in their big dam. Brenna and I yarn from time to time when we bump into each other, and I trade my mandarins for her eggplant. The neighbourliness is nice.

You could live around here for a lifetime and not meet half the residents. But people are my passion. So I let our newsagent Greg talk me into joining the community group's committee as publicity officer. Greg's the chairman.

At my first meeting, I am surprised to find that I already know a handful of the committee members. Nicky, the woman who led the river walk, is here and so is this bloke who makes terrific furniture, Dave.

As I walk into the room, he grins at me. 'I know you,' he says, pointing at me. 'Beer chair.'

'Yes,' I laugh, 'you're right. How are you?'

Dave shares a studio with his artist wife Pam and, before Christo came up here permanently, I dropped in one day for a sticky-beak. Every piece of furniture was a work of art in perfect balance, exquisite design showcasing the richness of the timbers he uses.

'Would you do me a favour?' Dave said with a broad smile. 'Take a seat and tell me what you think the chair's purpose is.'

He motioned to a spindle-back armchair and I sat, contemplated and pronounced, 'It's a beer chair, a great chair for drinking a beer.'

Dave laughed heartily. 'A beer chair. Yes. Come into the house and meet Pam.'

Pam was working on a series of fabric artworks depicting the frailty of several ethnic groups and their craft by telling their stories in immaculate stitchery and calligraphy.

I left their home inspired.

And now here's Dave at the SPADCO meeting. Seeing him and Nicky, being part of this group, signals the beginning of new relationships. We start having our car serviced by Darren, a third-generation local who works mechanical magic in his big old tin shed; I relinquish my dependence on my Sydney hairdresser and make an appointment ('I can fit you in next week, if you like') at Sharen's salon at the Point ($25 a haircut, and a good one at that); Rob, who sharpens anything and everything (unless the surf's up), revives our kitchen knives, secateurs and the chainsaw.

At Easter we're delighted by an unexpected invitation to brunch with Nicky and her scientist husband Geoff, who househusbands their daughter Mallee and bakes sourdough bread … with a starter dough given to him by Damon (our rainforest-organising Damon), who's here with his partner Shaz and making hollandaise sauce and tells us he builds bread ovens too.

Pam and Dave Jones are here, close friends apparently, and we meet Nicky's amazing mother Adrienne, one of the prime movers in getting the Sydney Paralympics off the ground in 2000. When Adrienne decided, in her sixties, to leave her long-time home in Sydney's northern beaches she jumped in boots and all — and bought a working mango farm, with one thousand trees. Unlike us, she kept working it.

'To be honest, love,' she confides with mock innocence, 'I didn't know what I was getting myself into. But … here I am.' Ade, as we quickly learn to call her, is SPADCO's secretary and now a good friend.

The meal stretches to four hours over a feast of chunky fresh fruit salad, jugs of freshly squeezed orange juice, baskets piled high with homemade muffins and eggs benedict made with our hosts' free-range eggs, ham and served with hollandaise on toasted home-baked sourdough.

And as we sort through issues of politics, the environment and surfing conditions, Christo and I discover some amazing connections with the people around the table. Dave Jones is a bushwalking mate of Doug Hocking from Orange … and we know Doug and his wife Jude from parties with our teacher friends Diane and John … and the Hockings know Andrew and Kerry, who live along Grassy Head Road … and Kerry went to school with Maggie, Theo's late, loved wife … and I have known Theo and Maggie for a good forty years.

Through SPADCO I also come to understand the wider community, learn of the need for better medical services for the locals, about half of them elderly; I hear fears that the community will be swamped by development if sewerage comes to Stuarts Point, and the opposing view that the stench of sewerage after heavy rains cannot be tolerated by those afflicted by it, or the river's pristine integrity; I see young parents struggling with poverty but determined to do the best for their kids, and other people's; I fence-sit about the huge B-double transports that rumble right through the village to reach the potato and avocado farmers. (Are these giant trucks safe on our village streets? ... Can you deny a farming bloke the means of making his living?)

I am part of this small, delicately balanced world now. What's my contribution to be, living alongside the children, the old folks, the surfers, the fishermen, the poets, the shopkeepers, the avocado pickers? This is my home, too.

My mother found she had breast cancer in August 2002 after her annual mammogram, but typically kept the news from her three daughters until she had tasted the fear, swallowed it and could be sure it had broken down in her system. Then she phoned and, in matter-of-fact tone, described the path she would follow: a lumpectomy, radiation treatment. At her age, then seventy-eight, and after initial exploratory tests, the doctors had said it was unlikely to be fatal; she was looking forward to having it dealt with so she could return smartly to Griffith University and complete her third degree, honours in Fine Arts. We were not to worry. Had we all been for our mammograms? Yes, Mum.

The treatment went according to plan, she was fine, but she didn't return to uni. Her new focus was to get well and strong and she tackled it with her usual determination until depression knocked her for six. Her next target was to get off the happy pills that made her sleep twelve hours a day. She beat the anti-depressants, too, after three half-forgotten years.

During my next visit to Sydney to work with the *Cosmo* girls, I have an unsettling experience: my left nipple starts feeling strange. An uncomfortable tingling sensation that comes on during the morning and persists all day. Once or twice I wriggle around in my chair, adjusting the way I'm sitting to see if that helps, but it doesn't;

surreptitiously, I try rubbing my breast hard with the heel of my hand. That's better.

After Mum's brush with cancer, I'm a little more anxious about my breasts than I used to be. And BreastScreen NSW has stepped up my free two-yearly mammograms to annual checks now that I have a 'family history'.

Cosmo is on deadline this week so I'm flat out at work, which distracts me, but the stinging feeling returns the next day.

Don't be foolish, I say to myself. Go and have it checked out today.

It's nothing, I argue back.

Well, it might be. Go and have it checked out. It could save your life.

It's really, really uncomfortable no matter how much I jiggle around in my bra and I am starting to feel uneasy, but ... it'll be all right.

Go and see the bloody doctor!

Okay, Okay. But first ... I head for the toilets, find an empty cubicle, strip off my shirt and give my breast a good hard rub. No relief. I remove my bra, inspect my nipple, prod around a bit, but fail to find anything that shouldn't be there.

Bugger. So I start to get dressed, pick up my bra and ... there, half hidden in the middle of the seam, is a small, prickly black cobbler's peg.

Ha! Mum doesn't have cancer and I don't either.

After work, I take the bus to Sydney Uni near where I'm staying and walk up Arundel Street to the Forest Lodge pub. I'm going to celebrate. This is my favourite inner-city pub. It used to carry a shingle bearing a painting of a cow and the words 'your country pub in the city' but, well, everything changes. Now it's simply the Forest Lodge Hotel.

Fortunately the ambience doesn't seem to have changed: uni students counting out the exact change for their happy-hour beers, locals who have lived around here for ever in cramped terraces, the lively Tuesday trivia night crowd, the Tuesday $6 pasta crowd, the noisy pool players, the overburdened backpackers, the TAB punters transfixed to the telly, the blank-faced pokies addicts. I sit at the bar drinking a cider, perfectly at ease in this community of strangers, absorbing their aura of belonging and, finding it familiar, missing Grassy.

Two drinks and I'm done, strolling back down Arundel past the back of the morgue. I stop in front of an attached brick cottage where a twiggy Christmas bush in the middle of a garden bed is battling gamely through the Sydney smog, and smile. I have to stop myself nodding. Its owner wouldn't understand how the sight of it takes me home.

Good news the day I'm to return to Grassy: at last someone has fallen in love with our Bondi Junction house and makes us an offer we can't really refuse although it's significantly lower than we had expected. Selling up represents the final break with our Sydney life. The cobbler's peg in my bra must have been a sign.

The pleasure of coming home is indescribable. I'm excited about seeing how the rainforest is going. I want to get back into my kitchen. I've missed Bindi.

'She's fine,' Christo assures me. 'But I can't keep her out of the dam.' He's been brushcutting the weeds around our plants and where he goes, she follows. 'Got a couple of ticks off her last night … oh, I think I told you.'

He did. We talk every day when we're apart.

Christo tells me Greg (the newsagent) has invited us to go kayaking with him and a mate on Sunday.

'Bring Janet along if she'd like the day out,' he told Christo.

'I want to show her the river. It's all silting up and we need something done about it.'

Not a problem. Janet is delighted at the chance to have a morning on the water and she's already there when we arrive at the boat ramp.

Some hot 1940s swing music is playing. A big band. Could be Glenn Miller.

'It's the senior cits,' Greg says. 'Every second Sunday they hold a dance in the hall.'

He introduces us to Robbo while untying the boats in the back of the ute. Robbo's from a grape-growing family out west, but his skills and background brought him across the divide and he now manages macadamia and mango plantations at Grassy for a Sydney couple.

It's not easy to find work when you're getting on, he tells Christo. Robbo must be all of fifty-five.

'Tell me about it,' Christo grins. After a bit of a yak, the two men click.

We set off up the river, towards Grassy Head and the spit of sand blocking the river. Robbo and I pair up, Greg takes Janet and Christo scores the single kayak.

Along the secluded reaches, where in places the water is less than 30 centimetres deep, we glide over swaying forests of sea grass. Tiny fish flick in and out of shadow, manta rays flatten themselves on the golden sand and crabs, some big enough to eat, scurry for cover.

Quiet as we are, even the flocks of black swans are wary of our approach and turn gracefully as one, webbed feet churning away beneath the surface, and set sail for a farther shore.

We stay to the left, passing landmarks we'd seen the day of the river walk: thickets of mangrove, the wooden landing, huge slabs of rock jutting from the water. Here, at a place on the river known as Razorback Point, is where we stop to beach the kayaks.

'Up here's the pilot station, the first one on the Macleay,' Greg calls, scrambling up a slope to the footpath we'd trodden this time last year. Tentatively we climb the narrow, steep steps that were hewn from rock in the 1860s, grabbing at scraggy saplings for balance as the rough-edged stairs twist up the northern face of Razorback Ridge. Before the 1893 flood, this is where Alexander McKenzie and his crew would come to maintain the flag mast as cargo-laden ships approaching the mouth of the Macleay manoeuvred around a blind spot known as Double Corner.

'There's not a lot of the station left to see,' Greg explains as we haul ourselves up the last step to the top of the ridge. The plateau is about the size of an average house, its sides dropping away sharply, and it's rocky underfoot. But the views over the ocean and back to Yarrahapinni are spectacular.

McKenzie is long gone, there are no artefacts left. But irreplaceable old-growth forest — eucalypts, black butt and brushbox — remains defiantly on top of the ridge and all the way down Razorback's southern side.

Robbo gives Christo a call a couple of nights after our paddle. 'Listen, mate. You reckon you're looking for work, anything within reason?'

'Yeah, that's right.' I can hear the excitement in his voice and edge closer, trying to work out who's on the phone.

'I've got some nuts that need picking and I'm a man short. What are you doing tomorrow?'

'Hey, that sounds great, Robbo. What time and where?' He grabs for a pad and writes. 'Fantastic. Yeah. See you there.'

'Guess what?' Christo turns to me. 'I start work tomorrow picking macadamias. Robbo needs an extra hand for a few days.'

'Great. What time do you start?'

'He's going to pick me up on Grassy Head Road at 7.15 am. I guess I'll be working until mid-afternoon.'

The news has an electrifying effect on me; not just that there's some work at last, but that someone is giving Christo a go. Who cares what the hourly rate is, this is a real job.

Next morning Christo boards Robbo's ute togged out for hard labour and I arrange to pick him up at the corner later, but he gets an early mark and is already walking up our road, Esky swinging, when I drive down to meet him.

'Oh, my back,' he groans, easing himself into the passenger's side.

'Was it very hard?'

'Oh, babe, you wouldn't believe how hard it is bending down all day to pick nuts up off the ground. And look at my arms and legs.'

He's covered in long scratches etched in stippled trails of dried blood, with a particularly nasty tear on his left cheek, just under his eye.

'I'll be wearing long sleeves tomorrow. And I'll remember to take some tea. Boy, I hurt.' Despite his wounds and healthy tiredness, Christo is elated and, after a few yoga stretches, a shower and two cuppas, he stretches out lengthwise on our faded old chesterfield and falls asleep.

Day two as a farm labourer is more of the same, yet with its own unique twist. This time, as he was reaching high into the trees to harvest the stone-hard nuts, he grabbed a hidden paper wasp nest.

'Let me tell you,' he says, holding his swollen red hand up to my concerned face. 'They sting!'

By the third day, Christo is on a roll. The work takes him to several different plantations, he helps with the sorting, picks up a few tips about harvesting and enjoys the camaraderie of his co-workers, a young fella called Nathan and a bloke named Bill.

His next adventure occurs on the fourth day when the trio is picking nuts on low branches — the worst job of all.

Christo stands for a minute to stretch, then sits on an inviting soft bale of hay.

'Shit,' Bill yells. Christo looks down to see a startled metre-long brown snake slither out from between his legs and head straight for Bill's trouser leg. At once, all three men leap to their feet, laughing with relief as the frightened snake disappears. (Christo and I are starting to get the message: snakes like hiding in mulch. But it will take one more scare …)

The morning of the fifth day is frosty and damp. And this day is a real doozy, my husband's last day of farm-labouring for a living — ever.

He phones around 9.30 am. 'Off to a great start today, babe. Like a fool, I fell out of the ute.'

'Oh, dear. How? What happened?'

'The ute pulled up on the hill where we were going to work but it hadn't quite stopped when I got up. My feet shot out from under me. I pitched head first out of the ute.'

'Are you okay?'

'Bit winded,' he tells me, in typical understatement. 'It could have been worse. Don't worry. I'll see how I feel at lunchtime.'

I'm not convinced he's really all right and, after a few minutes, I call back. 'Do you want me to come and pick you up?'

The relief in his voice is touching. 'You know, I think I would.'

With bruised ribs and ego, he waits at the farm gate until I come to collect him. 'I think I might have broken a rib,' he confesses, wincing as he clambers in. 'Maybe I'd better go to the doctor tomorrow.'

After a broken night of painful sleep, we set off to Christo's new GP in Nambucca, half an hour away. I'm driving, of course, carefully swerving to avoid ruts and rocks on the road so I don't hurt the patient. Gently I take the curve around the packing shed where Greg's hanging bananas. I edge up the crest and past the mango tree, taking it slowly I ease back into second gear as I cross the cattle grid when …

'Christ, look out!'

Instinctively I slam on the brakes as Christo lurches forward, yelling in pain. An enormous branch has fallen across the track.

Turning to Christo, I see he's smiling through a grimace of pain. The seat belt must have hurt his ribs.

'Guess I'll be late for the doctor,' he says wryly.

'Yep.'

'Great excuse, but, hey?'

So back up the hill we go for the chainsaw. Luckily Greg comes to help, cutting through the massive obstruction with a few well-placed strokes while Christo watches helplessly, nursing his ribs. I think it's time I learned to use the chainie.

'Now the money is in the bank and your tax bill has been paid,' Christo says, pouring me a plunger coffee, 'we can buy the tractor'. Like most major issues, we bring the discussion to the lunch table on the veranda. The green plastic table that was the centrepiece of our dining room in the early days here eventually flew across the veranda in a summer storm and cracked down the middle. We still have the chairs, but these days we eat at a stylish setting we bought to make the Bondi Junction house look attractive for sale.

The day is far too dreamy for drama-filled discourse so we mull over the options in leisurely fashion with sandwiches of homemade pesto, seed avocado (they're really not too bad) and cheese.

So. Tractor or ride-on? This is the first decision we have to make, and for weeks we've been talking about it, going round in circles. Well, I have anyway.

Are we serious about becoming real farmers — in which case we probably need a workhorse for slashing and ploughing, or whatever. Or will a good solid ride-on be sufficient for the flat areas (not that there are many of those) — in which case we'll hire someone to do the death-defying inclines. One thing we are sure of and that is that the you-beaut mower isn't going to be of any long-lasting help; as soon as one bit's mowed another is grassed over. In fact the poor old mower, which would last at least ten years on a backyard lawn, has to be on full throttle all the time now and even then makes a terrible revving noise as it chews at the Rhodes grass and Scotch thistle. The brushcutter is a Herculean tool, but it was never meant to clear a property our size week after week.

One advantage of a ride-on is that it's much cheaper. We've looked at zero-turn mowers with handles like ski poles and perfect turning circles so you don't have to back up, as you do with most ride-ons; but they aren't good on hills, says one expert. There's the sturdy Cox, a red ride-on manufactured and sold with national pride; its advantage is reliability, parts are readily available and … it's Australian made. Then we come to the green-and-gold John Deere 'lawn tractor', referred to by everyone (except dealers) as Dear John. American, classy, with four-wheel drive … and, it's true, much dearer than either of the others.

'I think,' Christo says, finishing his coffee, 'that we're better off getting a tractor because it can do more. A ride-on is just a mower. With a tractor we can buy accessories to do other jobs.'

As usual, Christo has managed to find clarity within the confusion.

So. Which tractor? Where do we start? Although we have shied away from the idea of a cheap second-hand tractor because of our total lack of mechanical knowledge, we've heard of a bloke who does up old Kubotas 'like new'.

Our estate agent mate Paul likes the Kubotas. 'I've had mine twenty-five years, bought it second-hand and wouldn't trade it for anything,' he declares unequivocally.

'Well, shall we start by ringing the Kubota man?' I ask Christo. 'Are you happy to consider a second-hand tractor?'

'If this bloke's got a good reputation and the tractor comes with some kind of warranty and follow-up service, yeah. I'd be into that. And parts. Ask him how easy it is to get parts.'

So I call the Kubota man. (The reason it's me making the call is that Christo hates phones. Says he's phonaphobic. I, on the other hand, have been known to talk for more than an hour to friends, no worries.)

'A friend has recommended your reconditioned Kubotas. Would you have one at the moment?'

'Actually, I'm not doing up tractors any more.'

'Oh. Would you know anyone who might have a Kubota for sale?'

'Nah. Can't say I do. What are you after?'

'Well, a tractor for our farm. It's a banana farm, pretty hilly, so a four-wheel drive.'

'Yeah, but what size?'

'Oh, not very big. Like, we're not planning to do any really heavy work. Just slashing and jobs around the farm. Umm … we haven't exactly bought a tractor before.' As if he hasn't worked that out already.

'So … what … about 30 horsepower?'

'Er … yeah … '

'Look, I don't know anyone at the moment. Let me think … no. Is it a Kubota that you're after especially?'

'No, just lots of people reckon it's a good tractor. Would it be better than a John Deere?'

'Hah. Dear John.' No one seems able to resist the joke.

'Aren't they worth the money?'

'Oh, yeah, they're a good tractor. You could have a look at the Ferguson, too.'

'What would they cost, d'you think?'

'Umm … oh … about $22,000, around there somewhere.'

'Twenty-two … I see. Er, do you know anyone who has a Massey Ferguson for sale?'

'No, not really. You could try Wauchope.'

'Is a Massey Ferguson better than a Kubota? Or a John Deere?'

'No, look, they're all good tractors. Depends what you want it for.'

Aaaagh. But we don't know what we …

'Ah, okay, thanks for your help, mate. We'll keep looking. Thanks again.'

I hunt out Christo, who's sharpening his cane knife on a stone. Very impressive.

'The Kubota bloke hasn't got one but he reckons we need about 30 horsepower and we should look at Fergies, too.'

'Where do they sell those?'

'He didn't say.'

We might as well be shopping for a skyhook.

In the end, after treks to Kempsey and Wauchope and Nambucca and Coffs, and considering big tractors, small tractors, tractors for hire (delivered to your door), tractor-plus-man for hire, reconditioned tractors, Korean tractors and many more we didn't see, read about or have recommended, it comes down to the largest John Deere small tractor. The JD has a good name, extra-wide cutting deck (62 inches or about 158 centimetres) perfect for orchards, excellent safety features (if your bum lifts off the seat for a second the motor stops), four-wheel drive plus a large orange button you kick if you lose traction and (the clincher that reassured me) Jim has one just like it but a bit bigger. Say goodbye to $17,000.

The John Deere dealer from Frederickton brings it up in his truck and gives it a whirl around the big yard. Christo pays earnest attention to all the details about safety and maintenance and mounts the gleaming tractor with a smile that swamps his entire face. Up and down the big yard he drives, sitting high in the bright yellow seat as the blades underneath spit out a stream of weeds from the bright yellow chute.

After the dealer has gone, Christo drives up beside me, brakes, spreads his arms wide and then tilts his hat back so the brim sits high. He begins to sing: 'Oh what a beautiful morning, Oh what a beautiful day.' Bloody idiot. I can't stop laughing. No wonder I love him.

'Give me a go, Christo.' The urge is so strong, it brings back childhood memories of fighting with Janet over whose turn it was on the trike.

'No, no, don't get on that side. Always mount on the left.'

'Just like a horse.'

'No, actually. Look over here and you'll see the right side has a rubber cover protecting the blades. It's not good to put your weight on it.'

He runs through the instructions, most of which I forget instantly in all the excitement, then I start to move forward slowly. This … is … so … much … fun! Getting faster and faster (its top speed is only 14 kilometres per hour), making circles in the grass around the grapefruit tree, zigzagging across to the still uninhabited chook house, a childlike silliness wells up inside me. I'm the queen of the mountain. I never, ever want to get down.

'Oh, God, no! Christo-o-o-o.'

'What? What's the matter?' He comes tearing outside to where I'm sitting on the ramp, nursing Bindi in my lap.

'She can't walk.'

Bindi looks up as he squats beside us, raising her head with great difficulty so she can lick Christo. 'It can't be a tick,' Christo says, 'it's only June. I thought the tick season started in August.'

Me, too. We have been so vigilant, Christo raking her coat with his fingers every day, peering into her grimy ears (a true act of affection), even inspecting her impenetrably bushy tail. Besides, the treatment to protect her from ticks and fleas is up to date.

Nevertheless, she has all the alarming signs of tick paralysis: her breathing is laboured and she collapses when she tries to stand.

I run my hands over her body, probing for the telltale lumps that are so difficult to see on her dense, dark coat.

'I've got one!' I cry. 'On her shoulder.' Bindi hasn't a clue what I'm excited about, but her ears prick up.

'Christo, get the hook. Quick.' He runs back inside for the two-pronged device we bought from the Sydney vet who treated her first tick paralysis but never used.

'Do you remember what to do?' He hands me the green plastic hook, then immobilises Bindi in a headlock. But there's no fight left in her.

'I think so. Which way are we supposed to twist this bloody thing?' If I get it wrong and leave the tick's head embedded in her flesh, the poison will keep pumping into her system.

'Anticlockwise. Three times.'

It sounds so, so … witchcrafty.

'Are you sure?'

'Yes. Just do it.'

I turn it once, twice, three times. The engorged parasite comes away caught firmly in the hook, its body a ghastly grey and the deadly pincers wriggling.

Bindi lifts her head, inquisitive as ever as I squash the tick vengefully on the concrete ramp, watching with pleasure as the blood spurts out.

Christo strokes her face, rubs her ears. 'C'mon, Stumblebum, let's get you to the vet.'

It's two nerve-racking days before Bindi pulls through, touch-and-go. She needs rest, warmth and small meals of soft food. Her heart has suffered, the vet tells us. He recommends another tick repellent, a tablet every second day, but warns it's extremely strong and might put more strain on her heart. We go with the advice. If she gets another tick now, it will kill her.

chapter thirteen

'Some mistakes are too much fun to only make once.'

Anonymous

Up along Fisherman's Reach as far as you can go is a fishing spot they call the Golden Hole. Long before the 1850s, when Kempsey people took pleasure cruises to the thriving settlement of Stuarts Point on board *The Olga* and settlers held picnic races along the beach at Grassy Head on New Year's Day, the area around here was a sacred Aboriginal place. Here, where the Macleay and Clybucca Creek merge, the waters teemed with flathead, black fish and the ugly crocodile long tom, carpets of plump oysters clung to the rocks and muddies and sand crabs scavenged the plentiful shallows.

Aboriginal tribes would gather here from the mountains, from the south and from the north to feast on seafood and the sweet nuts of the bunya.

When the white newcomers discovered it, they called it the Golden Hole.

Janet and I are sitting on the porch of the waterfront unit she's renting for a few days at the Stuarts Point Holiday Park, getting into a sauvignon blanc. Or rather I am. She's been working.

'I was thinking,' says my sister the mayor, pushing aside a stack of papers for some meeting she has to go to next week. 'We haven't been fishing for ages. Now that it's stopped raining at last, let's go up and try the Golden Hole. I've never been fishing up there.'

'If you like. But they reckon the fishing's no good there anymore,' I reply. 'Greg told me — the newsagent. There was a weir built there in the 1970s to reclaim the land and he says it ruined the fishing.'

Janet stashes her papers in a briefcase on the floor, then splashes wine into her empty glass. A group of barefooted local kids run past on their way to the beach, a panting bitser at their heels.

'I know what they say but you're fishing with me, right, and I catch fish.' It's true. Only yesterday she'd bagged a decent-sized sole off the footbridge. I've never even had a bite there.

From across the river, washed pink in the early evening light, a large flock of yellow-tailed black cockatoos screeches towards the trees down at Fisherman's Reach. They say black cockies signal rain. But we've already had seven straight days of it — our driveway is a mess, criss-crossed with rain-gouged furrows. Despite Mark's efforts to smooth it out with his big tractor it's so bumpy and slippery we have to drive in second gear.

Janet fills my glass. 'Since there seems to be a break in the weather, why don't we go tomorrow afternoon. I'll bring some bubbly and meet you there. Don't worry about bait, I've got everything we need.'

Fortunately the rain holds off the next day, although there's a bit of cloud massing in the east.

Christo's decided to come with us although he doesn't like fishing, and I won't let him help. Last time, in our newlywed days, he managed to drop a large bream I'd just caught … back into the water. As I watched the bream bob out to sea, the fact that he was being gallant and removing the hook from its mouth at the time didn't make me feel any better.

'Of course I'm coming.' He sounds offended that I'd think otherwise. 'I haven't been to the Golden Hole. And I like being around you.' He grins. 'I won't touch your fishing rod.'

There's bitumen all the way from the Point to the boat ramp at Fisherman's Reach, where a car ferry operates to Freedom Island; Freedom Island used to be known as Shark Island, something I always bear in mind.

Beyond the boat ramp, the road varies from graded gravel, rutted tracks to tyre marks on flattened grass until eventually it runs out at sandy beaches strewn with driftwood and shells. The road is passable all the way in two-wheel drive as long as it's dry, but it's fairly boggy in spots today so I'm glad we're in the truck.

Janet grins and waves as we park beside her mayoral vehicle, a four-wheel drive like ours but showroom-fresh.

'What kept you?' she calls. In sarong and thongs, with no makeup, it's unlikely any ratepayers will recognise her. Not that there's a soul here but us.

The tide is high and beginning to ebb. Clybucca Creek, tumbling and frothing as it enters the mouth of the Macleay Arm, sweeps past the narrow strip of beach where Janet is fishing. This confluence is the legendary Golden Hole.

While Janet fills a plastic glass with bubbly, I poke around in the bait bucket for a worm — might be some whiting around.

Christo gets a beer from our Esky. 'I'm going to have a look at the weir.'

'Okay, love.' Janet and I wave at his disappearing back.

'Any bites?' I ask Janet.

She has two lines going, the rods stashed in holders buried in the sand to leave her hands free so she can have a smoke.

'Hold your horses. I've only been here for fifteen minutes.' She pours me a drink while I bait my hook, and I take it in my left hand so I don't smear the stem with my wormy fingers.

'You know you oughta give them up.'

Her eyes never leave her fishing rods. 'Nothing worse than a reformed smoker.'

'Yeah, well … ' I don't like preachers, either, but she and Rosie are my prime anti-smoking targets. I want them both to grow old with me.

We both fall silent. The wind is freshening, not a good omen for fishing.

I walk along the sand, stepping over clumps of white-parched driftwood to find a spot of my own, and cast with the wind.

'Nothing doing over here,' I call to her after a while. 'Not a sausage. How about you?'

A shake of her head. 'Let's try farther down.'

Together we carry the bait bucket and Esky to a spot closer to the weir. 'So, why did they gate the creek?'

'The plan was to reclaim the wetlands to improve the land for farming. It never happened. The drainage didn't really get any better, there was no rush to farm it and we lost about 100 hectares of mangroves. No mangroves, no fish.'

'So what are we doing fishing here?'

'For Pete's sake … Enjoying the beauty of our surroundings,' she replies in mock frustration. You'd think she was the big sister. We sit down on the gritty sand, our thoughts drifting with our lines as the tide pulls away.

From the right we hear the dull chug-chug of a boat that slowly emerges from behind some mangroves, a flat-bottomed vessel with two men on board. They steer into a narrow inlet opposite us and, with the motor idling, one man hauls up a crab net dripping with sea grass. He stows it in the bow. Even though the light is fading, I can see he has at least one crab clicking crankily in the net. Then the boat moves on along the line of mangroves, edging into another inlet and vanishes from view.

I must buy that crab net … and a tinnie.

Christo's come back, runners covered in mud.

'Did you find the midden?' Janet asks.

'No. Didn't know there was one.'

'It's a fair way up and it'll be pretty boggy up there. The midden is supposed to be the longest one in the Southern Hemisphere.'

Suddenly she jumps to her feet. 'See that.' The tip of her rod is jerking in staccato bursts. 'Got a bite. A good one.'

Carefully lifting her rod from the holder, she plays out

the line, allowing it to run over her right index finger so she can sense the slightest movement. Rat-a-tat-tat, goes the line. And again.

'Damn. Think I've lost my bait.' Slowly she winds in her good old Alvey. No fancy modern eggbeater reel for Janet, she's been fishing with Alveys all her life.

'Yep. Bait's gone. Small bream probably.'

Janet casts again. 'That'll be my last of the day.' The mozzies have started to descend on us.

Christo's having another beer, exploring the beach.

'Getting back to the weir,' she says to me, 'you'll be pleased to know that something is happening about that. There is a program to rehabilitate the wetlands and we're after some state government funding right now.'

We start packing up. The fishing will probably improve as night descends, but the mozzies have beaten us.

Christo and I drive off first, taking a wide arc across the grass and through a large muddy patch to get back on the track. Janet follows: across the grass, into the mud and … stops. She's bogged. Tyres spin and black mud flies, but she's going nowhere but down. The vehicle is up to its axle in mud.

The usual solutions are tried and fail: rocks under the wheels simply sink into the mire, sheets of rusty tin roofing that have been dumped nearby crumble, fallen branches squelch to one side.

It's dark now, and starting to rain. Things are looking pretty hopeless.

When it comes to the crunch, there are some people you can always count on to solve a problem with commonsense and quiet determination.

'I'm going home for the chain we used to pull that big log up the hill,' Christo says. 'Be back as soon as I can. I ought to be able to pull you out.'

The rain's pelting down and it's black as pitch out here. The Golden Hole is a miserable place to be when you're stuck in the mud, the mozzies are biting and your stomach's rumbling.

But Christo returns after an hour with the chain and in surprisingly good humour considering the fate that awaits him.

'Well, here I go.' Lying in the mud, he attaches the chain to Janet's vehicle.

'That's one,' Christo calls through the stinging rain as he loops the chain around the towing hook on our truck which is parked on higher ground.

'And that's the other.'

He pauses to scrape a layer of mud from his hands with a towel he brought from home, then wraps it around his ruined clothes and climbs back into our truck. 'Now … let's see.'

Filthy, slimy and absolutely drenched, Christo drags Janet's pride and joy from the muck.

'Thank you so much,' she calls out to him above the noise of the rain as she reaches solid ground. 'I'd hug you but … '

My hero laughs. 'Just one question, Janet. Did you go into four-wheel drive when we left the bitumen?'

Janet smiles coyly. 'Er … remind me. How does that work again?'

Jim reckons that all this rain so soon after planting is beginner's luck, for our rainforest is thriving. New shoots have appeared on most of the plants, and some are more than 30 centimetres tall already. I think Jim is secretly pleased for us; he's fully aware of how much he and Margaret have inspired us — not to mention the invaluable practical advice from Wendy and Chris.

But the rain has spurred on the weeds as well as our fledgling forest. It won't be long before they overtake the young trees.

'I'm going to have to spray soon, darling.' By unspoken consent, I am the appointed weed killer in the family. 'Can you make me that thing Damon drew for you, please.'

It's an ingenious device to protect plants from spray drift.

'Sure. It shouldn't be too hard to knock one up. I'll do it this afternoon.'

Christo's already scored an empty 20-litre plastic container from Greg, and commandeered a dowel rod I've been planning to use for a weaving project for, well, since Alix was born. The dowel is the perfect length — 1.2 metres.

He cuts the container in half diagonally from top to bottom, trims the top and bottom off one half and glues the dowel into the corner.

'There you go. Just let the glue set overnight and Bob's your uncle.' He demonstrates. 'Hold onto the dowel so, and place the plastic part on the ground to shield the plant on two sides. When you've sprayed, move the shield to the other side.'

Brilliant. What a handy tool.

Next day I'm down at the rainforest early, attacking the weeds with a vengeance, squirting them pink. Damon says weeds are the biggest threat to the survival of our natives and I regard anything we didn't plant as a weed.

One tank of spray lasts about an hour and covers about ten per cent of the area. Although the work is slow, I find it relaxing, almost meditative, to move up and down the winding rows on my mission.

However, I'm alert the whole time for wind shifts that might carry the spray past my shield. It would be disastrous to poison the trees.

I recognise many of the weeds, but can't name most of them, and find I'm automatically giving them labels of my own devising: the bad one with burrs that catch in Bindi's curls, the thin weak-looking one that's hard to pull out, the grass that grows flat on the ground. I hunt each of them down and deliver the poison, and before long the shield is as pink as my runners.

I learn three important lessons this morning. One: bending forwards with 16 litres of liquid in your backpack brings you unceremoniously onto all fours (best-case scenario). Two: squatting with aforesaid full tank and then trying to stand again will flip you onto your back, legs in the air, in an instant. Three: it's always tricky, and sometimes painful, trying to get back up.

'Got a good business for you in Kempsey.' Paul, the real estate agent, is on the phone. We've been matey with him since we bought Grassy and he's popped in a couple of times when he's been in the area. He knows we don't want to have to keep going to Sydney for work.

'Oh, yeah. What is it?'

'A fish and chip shop, the only one in town.'

Fish and chip shop. Hmmm … I like the sound of that.

'It's a good business, good returns, and the fish and chips aren't bad. As a matter of fact, I get lunch there most Fridays. Would you like to have a look at it? No obligations, of course.'

Where have I heard that line before?

Christo's eyebrow arches when I tell him. 'Yeah, I'd be in that.' I'm surprised, but call Paul back and arrange to meet him at the fish and chip shop for lunch on Friday.

By the time Christo and I reach Kempsey, we're keyed up with excitement. Running a café has been an idea we've shared, along with the fantasy of an alp by the sea.

'Three fish and chips, please.' Paul orders the meal while we find a vacant table with a good view of the kitchen. The place is filling up fast.

'Of course you'd want to put your own touches on it,' Paul says, bringing cappuccinos that have somehow been created from an urn of boiling water.

I'm only half listening, too busy imagining where I'd arrange the tables and chairs, painting the walls blue, adding potted plants. We would ask staff to stay on at least until we learned the ropes …

The woman behind the counter is calling out our order number; if we buy it, we will have table service. Christo will be front-of-house and the staff will wear smart black polos. We will cook in oil, not animal fat.

'Well, what do you think?' Paul is squeezing lemon onto his battered fish, which he's broken into two steaming pieces.

From me: 'Loads of potential.' The chips are good but I think the batter should be lighter.

From Christo: 'Can we see the books?' He's only managed to eat a bit more than half of the huge serving.

The owner has spotted us with Paul, and worked out we're potential buyers. He watches us closely as we walk away in the direction of the real estate office.

I can't wait to get home to look through the profit-and-loss statements, and eagerly open the envelope while Christo starts the car.

'Before we go too far,' Christo says sensibly, 'we should ring Garry'. The accountant. 'I love the idea of owning a fish and chip shop, but let's get advice first.'

Strangely, Garry's reaction is very much the same as Janet's was when I told her. 'What on earth do you want a fish and chip shop for?'

'Because we like the idea, and can see potential in the place. It might be fun.'

'Fun? You're joking, aren't you?' I had forgotten the hard-nosed focus of the Sydney professional class.

'Hard work, long hours. Your clothes will smell of fat.' We must be paying him by the second, I think.

'What's the turnover?' Garry's rock solid.

I run my finger down the columns of figures before me. 'Hang on a minute.' I find it and tell him.

'Wages bill?'

'Yeah, ummm … here it is.'

'Net profit over the past three years? SAV?'

'Pardon?'

'Stock at valuation. Is it included in the price? Equipment, etcetera.'

Details, details!

He falls silent, doing the calculations. I hold my breath.

'Forget it.' Just like that. Can't think outside the square.

'Forget it?'

'You'd be buying yourself a job and that's a bad idea. Start something of your own.'

Bloody accountants. No imagination!

But it has started us thinking again about having a café, maybe in the packing shed. It's pretty basic: no panes in the windows, a few floorboards missing, it leaks in parts and has only three walls. However, there's a flat area next to it where cars could park and it has atmosphere and views.

From the sagging windows, you can see the sea and our drive winding up through Margaret and Jim's blue quandongs and past the tall, grey stump of a dead tree where kookaburras perch as they search for prey.

We could serve espresso made from freshly roasted beans, my tuna empanada and Christo's minestrone. We would have art on the walls, live music and books people can read while they're having coffee.

I add the packing shed café to my list of dreams.

There's a move afoot to do something about the community hall at Stuarts Point.

'It's an eyesore,' says newsagent Greg. 'Visitors come to Stuarts Point and what they see at the end of the village is this uninteresting old building.'

Apart from the library users and the senior citizens, who have already added a small kitchen, Greg says it's underutilised. It's easy to see why.

The stairs at the side are unsteady, the handrail rusted and unsafe. The gate to the side yard doesn't close properly and is difficult to move. The old concrete rainwater tank, full no doubt but no longer used, squats stolidly behind the hall blocking the river view. Inside, the acoustics are so dreadful it's impossible to hear people speaking unless everyone else is silent.

As publicity officer for SPADCO, I'm asked to come up with some ideas to present to the next meeting which is being held in the library section of the hall. No worries.

After we've dealt with the minutes and correspondence, I announce my Big Plan. No beating around the bush, I get right to it.

'I think we should get everyone in Stuarts Point to help paint the outside of the hall.'

Looking up from my papers I realise I don't have the attention of everyone at the meeting yet, but I will.

'Not a solid colour. Let's get them to paint anything they like, a picture or even their name or initials on the side of the hall. Get the young people to 'tag' the concrete water tank (with friendly supervision, of course).'

Now they're listening. Their eyes have stopped roving around the library bookshelves and their fingers have ceased drawing doodles on their agendas.

'If they all make their mark, they'll feel ownership of it and want to be involved. The hall would have character, it would look bright and inviting. It would be noticed by everyone and people would start using it as a true community gathering point.'

I stop to catch my breath and scan the faces around me for reactions.

Dave clears his throat to speak.

'I think the idea has merit,' he says diplomatically and smiles at me, 'but maybe painting the entire hall would be too radical for some people. What if we just painted the rainwater tank?'

I see relief in the eyes of the committee members, who quickly applaud my enthusiasm and welcome Dave's interpretation. I'm a little disappointed. I've always been a big-picture person myself.

However, we've achieved the objective of creating more interest in the hall. The tank will be painted, with the guidance of a man who teaches art at the club.

Unfortunately, on the day of the working bee, I'm in Sydney but Christo's going to lend a hand.

I'm surprised to hear from him at around noon.

'How'd it go, love?'

'Okay. Looks pretty good but I came home early. They're doing fine without me.'

What is it he's not telling me?

'So … why did you come home early?'

'I cut my knee.'

'How?'

'On a broken stubby. I was painting around the back of the tank and knelt on a broken stubby.'

'Is it bad?'

'It'll be all right I guess. But it won't stop bleeding.'

'You should go to Macksville Hospital.'

'I can't. When I drive the blood pours out.'

For Pete's sake. What can I do from here? Aaah, I know …

'Janet, hi, it's me.' I tell her the story.

'Right. I'm on my way. Tell Christo I'll be at Grassy in half an hour to take him to the hospital.'

The wound needs four stitches and I make a promise never to volunteer Christo for community service again.

After being in Sydney for three weeks, I'm unbelievably excited about coming home. The 2.55 pm flight goes so quickly the attendants don't even have time to serve coffee.

On the drive from Coffs airport, I quiz Christo about what's been happening up here — petrol prices (still about 10 cents higher than Sydney), rainfall (none) and our forest (growing, and so are the weeds). Sounds as if I'll need to spray again before I go back to Sydney on Monday.

'It really is incredible how big some of the trees are now,' Christo says, slowing down abruptly on the outskirts of Urunga, where the speed limit is enforced so rigidly the local cops mustn't ever get a tea break.

I have news of my own. Alix's twenty-first birthday party in September is all under control. While I was down in Sydney we finalised all the details and booked a room at a New York bistro-style pub, the Three Weeds, in Sydney's Inner

West: a menu of olives, nuts and mixed gourmet pizza boards, beer and wine for our guests and dance music (nothing to do with the quick step or the tango).

'The only thing she's worried about now is that you will embarrass her in your speech.'

'Me?' There's playful wickedness in his tone.

'You'd better not. I told her not to worry.'

'I wouldn't dream of it,' he chuckles. 'Hey … wait 'til you see the lemons.' All the pruning I did in the first year has paid off, apparently.

It's getting dark when we arrive, but before going into the house I take a tour. On the lemon tree, one branch is so loaded with fruit it's dangling right to the ground; we'll have to tie it up.

It's taken two seasons for the lemon to recover from my severe pruning and crop like this. We'll be giving fruit away when it's ripe. What a change that will be. Our neighbours and Greg have been so generous to us in the past, now we can thank them in kind. Last time I was up, Jim gave us a magnificent jap pumpkin that we turned into soup and scones. And one day Michael and Irene arrived with a grafted peach tree. Sharing produce is one of the joys of living here, where our neighbours are pure gold.

In the dim light I can see that the navel orange tree is laden with fruit, too, and the mandarin, which will bear in a few weeks, is going to give us a bumper harvest.

Even the scrappy old lemonade tree has responded well to me cutting it back last year and we should have plenty of fruit for juice.

It's wonderful to be back. No deadlines, no uncomfortable city shoes, no traffic. Next morning I map out my time at home: weeding the rainforest takes priority, the citrus need more mulch, it's time to plant spinach and more beans.

My work clothes come out of the cupboard: jeans and

T-shirt, thick socks, my pink runners, safari hat.

'Before I go a-spraying, love, let's go and have a look at the orange tree Greg told us about.'

'Okay by me. It's absolutely covered in oranges.'

'Yeah, Greg said it was amazing. How come I've never seen it?'

'It was surrounded by the bananas.'

We follow one of the old banana tracks along the crest of our hill past the chook house and the Christmas bush. It's not part of the property I get to often, spending most of my time in the home orchard and vegie garden. 'See,' Christo points. 'Over there near the watering pole.' Since Greg killed off the bananas, the place is dotted with tall irrigation poles now acting as perches for Willie wagtails and kookaburras.

'It looks hard to get to.' I hesitate to trek through the Rhodes grass and instead turn to inspect the ocean. Two container ships are about to pass on the horizon, seemingly on a collision course. A lone sailor is tacking out from South West Rocks on a blinding sea.

'Must get down here on the tractor and do some clearing,' Christo remarks. 'I'll have to use the brushcutter first so I don't run over the irrigation pipe and whatever else might be here. C'mon. I'll go first.'

Bindi bounds after him. I reckon she'll scare off any snakes, but I still don't like walking through high grass when I can't see what's there.

'Most of the fruit is at the top,' he says, approaching the tree and searching its higher branches. 'We'll have to bring the avocado tool.'

Brian left it for us, a doover of his own invention: a long steel pole with a smallish faded red canvas bag at one end and a rope pulley arrangement attached to shears above the bag. Position bag and shears under the unreachable fruit, pull the rope to cut through the stem and the fruit falls into the bag — if you can get it to work, which I can't.

I have another idea. 'You know, we should prune it back after the oranges are finished so we can reach the fruit. Actually, we should prune all the fruit trees back.'

'Even the mango?' He means the one in the home orchard. The one down near the dam is definitely a cherry-picker job.

'Yep. The mango, the lychees … and I'll get you to get rid of the guava. We don't like the fruit, and they attract the fruit flies.'

These rotten pests are one of the hazards of living near the coast. They got to my tomatoes last summer and I suspect a few of the oranges were hit too. The small puncture wounds in the skin are a dead giveaway.

'If we can get rid of the guava there might be a chance to control fruit fly in the nectarine and peach trees.' It's a faint hope, really. If the fly doesn't get the fruit, the birds probably will, but I want to give it another try.

We pick a few oranges from the lower branches. I fold up my T-shirt into a makeshift apron so I can carry them back up to the house.

After the spraying and lunch, I start cleaning up in the shadehouse. Rosie and I had weeded under the nursery benches some weeks ago, leaving behind piles of mulchable plant material. The weeds were sprayed before we pulled them out, so they'll be fine to use on the garden; they're already starting to break down.

Forking the grass into the wheelbarrow feels good; the activity stretches my computer-cramped muscles and my spine. I'm going to dump this load on the mandarin tree, which is swamped in cobbler's pegs. I wheel it over, steady the first fork-load with my left hand and drop it in place. Three armloads does the job, but I see it's too close to the trunk and will cause collar-rot, so I bend over to scrape it away from the base.

Out pops the head of a venomous black snake. Screaming for Christo I run to the house but, of course, by the time he arrives the snake has gone.

I can only shake my head in disbelief. When will I ever learn?

chapter fourteen

'They have their own unique character
and are fun loving and mischievous.
They think for themselves, are sometimes
smarter than you and are clowns,
with more personality than other dogs.'

Airedale profile, dogzonline.com.au

People continue to ask us what we're going to do with the place, and our stock answer is that we're still thinking about it. Being in Sydney so much, first Christo and then me, has made it difficult to build up momentum or follow through an idea properly.

I don't see the greenhouse as a serious moneymaker. I've raised plenty of bromeliads and anthuriums (mostly because they're so easy to propagate), which make marvellous gifts, but that's about it.

As for the Christmas bush, another local who saw our trees said that, in his opinion, our best option was to dig them out and start again, which doesn't appeal to either of us. If it were simply a case of resurrecting them we could do it, but we didn't buy Grassy to become cut-flower growers.

One of the first websites I pored over in the early days was the Ag Department's, and the fact sheet on growing flowers stressed that it's bloody hard yakka.

Who knows: maybe we have another twenty years of fit and healthy life ahead of us. But the reality is that we aren't as robust as we were at thirty, and our lives and livelihood simply cannot depend on labour-intensive farming.

I have come to a conclusion about small farming enterprises: that it's the biggest career gamble a new chum can make. You're reliant on the right weather at the right time, as well as predicting which crops will be in demand next year or even years down the track. If you get sick, work stops until you get better.

Despite that knowledge, I still want to grow something that will make use of the land and bring us some income. But what?

Posting a letter one day, I run into Christo's erstwhile farm boss Robbo.

'G'day, Robbo, how's it going.'

'Not bad, not bad. How's it with you?'

'Oh, you know, trying to work out what to do with our place. What would you grow, Robbo?'

He doesn't even pause to consider. 'Don't farm,' he says bluntly. 'You're too old.'

'What about maccas? We've got a couple of macadamias and they seem to do all right. Plenty of nuts.'

'Your place is too hilly for maccas. Harvesting would be a nightmare.'

'Citrus, then? We have a north-facing slope that would be ideal.'

'You're spraying all the time with citrus. Forget it.'

'Mangoes?'

'You can grow them around here, but we're really too far south. Have you got any mango trees?'

'Yes, all over the property.'

'How was last season?'

'Well, they set fruit early on but we didn't get more than a dozen.'

'Off how many trees?'

'Couple.' Ten, as a matter of fact, but I won't admit that.

'What about the year before that and the year before that?'

I move on.

'Chillies? What about chillies, Robbo?'

'Look … What do you want to farm for, anyway? You're a writer, aren't you? Why don't you write?' I would say 'Johnny Appleseed' to him, but he wouldn't understand. Robbo is a proper farmer.

Over dinner I tell Christo about my conversation with Robbo.

'It's so frustrating,' I tell him. 'We have to do something. The more we clear, the more the weeds grow and we're going to go broke buying diesel for the bloody tractor. We can't spend our lives growing a few fruit and vegies and watching the whales go by.'

We've had this conversation several times before, but never with the clarity Robbo has brought to the discussion.

'Yeah, you're right. We just keep going around in circles.'

'What about native trees? You know, the more I think about it the more I feel confident farm forestry's the go. Our place is similar to Jim and Margaret's, same hilly terrain, so we know natives will flourish.'

'Yeah, well, I've always liked the idea of natives,' Christo responds, 'and they would certainly improve the value of the property. Mind you, Alix is the one who will benefit.' Some farm foresters say you can cull certain native trees at eight years, but it's more likely to be twenty years before the timber is ready for harvest around here.

'And if we don't plant something on those really steep slopes we'll have serious erosion problems,' Christo adds.

'It would be hard work getting them established but after a couple of years they would pretty well take care of themselves.'

I feel passion begin to surge, but …

'We don't want to lose our view, though, do we. We'll have to be selective about what we plant and where.' Brenna and Mark also wouldn't like it much if we planted a forest of trees that would reach 50 metres in height.

Christo agrees. At least we're settled on our plan. Farm forestry it is.

It's Alix's birthday tomorrow and I've come down to Sydney ahead of Christo, who wants to finish some slashing. I'm surprised I haven't heard from him yet today. He said he would ring when he was leaving, which he planned to do at around 10 am.

Just before noon, he phones.

'I can't find Bindi. Bloody dog.' He sounds more concerned than angry, though.

'What do you mean?' Foolish question.

'She won't come when I call her.'

'That's strange.'

'I've whistled until I'm blue in the face and I've walked right around the property calling to her. I don't know where else to look, but I can't wait any longer.'

'When's the last time you saw her?'

'This morning, when I came outside to start packing the truck. About 8 am. We had a nice chat and she wandered off somewhere, I dunno. I hate to go but … '

I don't want him to leave before he finds her either. What will she do when she gets back and no one is there?

'Will you leave out plenty of food and water?'

'Already done that. Look, we'll be back on Monday and I'm sure she'll be okay until then.' He doesn't sound very positive, but there's nothing else we can do.

'You're probably right.' My priority is Alix's party, but I can't stop thinking about Bindi. Crazy, impulsive dog that she is, she never strays far from home when Christo is there. She might chase after a ground bird, follow her nose down a wallaby trail or wade into the dam for a drink and a wallow, but when Christo's working outside she is always within coo-ee, frolicking and exploring.

Eventually I give in to my nagging anxiety and ring Brenna and Mark, who, because we don't have fences, are Bindi's extended family.

'I haven't seen her all day, Gillian. Hold on,' Brenna says, then calls out to Mark. 'Have you seen Bindi today? Perryn have you been playing with Bindi today?' The background voices don't sound encouraging.

'Gosh, I'm sorry, Gillian.'

'Never mind. She'll turn up. Would you mind calling me when she comes back to let me know she's okay? Christo has left food and water for her.' I give her my mobile number.

'I certainly will. Oh, I hope she's all right.'

'She will be.'

'The only thing I'm worried about, Mum, is that Dad will embarrass me in his speech tonight. Please ask him not to.' She looks so beautiful in her new shimmery top, short black shorts and black high heels, my throat catches.

Christo's yarning with John and Di, who've come all the way from Corowa.

'He won't embarrass you, love.'

'How do you know?'

'I just know. Don't worry.'

I know because I remember: I see him rocking her in his arms when she was ill, going down the slippery slide with her when she was frightened, helping with her homework until she decided it was perfect, reading her favourite bedtime stories night after night.

'He loves you too much.'

And indeed his speech is warm and witty and nostalgic … what can be heard of it above the loud music and laughter. He recalls her 'difficult' birth, the forceps delivery observed by a row of midwifery students, how he fell in love with our baby instantly. Our old friends are remembering too. We were young together once. Alix's friends munch their way through piles of gourmet pizza and drink bubbly and imported beer on tap, as Christo and I reminisce. We made it, the three of us. So far, so good.

At midnight, Alix and her friends go clubbing and, while Christo tries to hail a cab, I check my mobile.

Brenna hasn't called.

Driving home on Monday, all we can talk about is Bindi: whether she'll be there or not, why she didn't come when Christo called, what we will do if she's not .there. The anticipation is stomach-wrenching and, as we reach the end of our drive, our eyes are fixed on the veranda where Bindi always waits for us.

But she's not there. She doesn't come bounding over to the garage to welcome us home. She doesn't leap and dance to greet us. There is just a hole where she should be, a deafeningly empty gap.

The dish of food Christo left for her is untouched; even the rats haven't been at it. A solitary leaf drifts across the top of her water bowl, pushed along by a light sea breeze.

Christo silently unloads the car as I go inside to phone Brenna, but she has no news of the dog. They hunted for her after I rang, searched all over their place and ours, calling and whistling.

Perhaps someone stole her. Now that's possible; after all, she is a pure-bred dog and quite distinctive looking. Not to mention very friendly. Or she chased a wallaby, got lost and went home with someone she met.

Christo makes himself busy outside while I start phoning around. First is the vet to ask if she's been brought in. She hasn't. Then I ring Macksville pound, the nearest and therefore the most likely place someone would have taken her.

'What sort of dog is it?' the bloke on the phone, who says his name is Reg, asks.

'An Airedale terrier.'

'Oh.' He sounds sad. Maybe he knows something.

'Why did you say "oh" like that?' I'm saying to myself, please don't tell me she's dead.

'It's just Airedales are such lovely dogs. No, I haven't got her I'm afraid.'

Clearing my throat, I give Reg our contact details before trying the Frederickton pound and the RSPCA. But no luck.

On a sudden impulse, I ring the breeder in Victoria and tell him.

'She is such a beautiful dog. So playful and loving. I thought I would let you know. Maybe someone will find her and contact you.'

I'm sure he can hear me sniffling, but I don't mind. He's upset to hear she's gone missing too.

'Why not contact the Airedale club. You never know.'

'Yes, yes, I will. Thank you.' But I don't. Instead, I type a notice to put in the shop windows at the Point. Someone might have seen her.

Over the next couple of weeks, Christo and I get stuck into the weeds in the rainforest. The hard work is good therapy. The fast-growing trees are an impressive height already, taller than me, yet it's less than twelve months since we planted. It's a real thrill.

But every day without Bindi is bleaker; she haunts us while we work. I hear a splash from the dam and look up, expecting her to run up to us all black and smelly; a sudden movement catches my eye, but it's a wallaby edging across the rise; something thrashes about beyond the lantana, but it's the inquisitive Clydesdales trying to see who's on the other side of the fence.

One day, when we break for lunch up on the veranda, I talk to Christo about it, about half-seeing her everywhere;

it's the same for him. We are both bewildered by her disappearance and desolate.

'I think she went off to die,' Christo tells me. 'Thinking back, she was strange the night before she disappeared. She didn't seem at all interested in the bone I gave her so I checked her for ticks. But she didn't have any on her.'

He turns quickly away from me, blows his nose, stares into the distance.

'I let her down. I should have realised something was wrong and taken her to the vet … the last time I saw her she looked back at me for a minute and then just walked into the bush. I think she knew.' He wipes his eyes on the back of his hand.

'Don't say that.' I put an arm around him, feeling his silent sobs, and let my tears loose too. 'You loved her and looked after her. If she was sick, we didn't know.'

'I should have known. She was finding it harder and harder to walk up the hill lately, always panting.'

'Darling, whatever happened, it was not your fault.'

He shakes his head. 'I miss her.'

'I know.'

The next day, Christo puts her trampoline bed away in the garage. It's time to take down the notice in the shop windows. We have to face it … Bindi isn't coming home.

Having the tractor has made all the difference to managing the farm, so Christo is much more confident about our ability to stay on top of things. We've cleared and tidied along the drive from the mango tree up to the packing shed, making the entrance to the property inviting and quite park-like.

To our delight, we've come across a few pioneer plants fighting their way up from beneath fallen branches and weed growth — bleeding hearts, Sally wattles and tree ferns — and a silky oak. In fact, there are three silky oaks along the drive, one of which is going to have to go; it's that or damage the phone line. An avenue of silky oaks along the drive would be magnificent and since these three are apparently self-sown, they should prosper here. Good for stopping erosion, too.

The clean-up has also uncovered a cool, sheltered gully where Bangalow palms and tree ferns are thriving and the deep-throated chorus of frogs resounds.

Christo has been slashing the overgrown tracks Greg hasn't used for months, pushing back the weeds and reclaiming more and more of the land so we can see where we're going and what's what. Now that we've had a roll bar fitted to the tractor, Christo plans to tackle some of the less daunting slopes. I'm not sure about this. Last time I was in Sydney he managed to bring down the Hills hoist with the roll bar when he tried to mow under it, snapping it off at the base and reconfiguring one spoke so it now has a permanent elbow.

I don't know if Christo is accident-prone or just bloody unlucky, but I've begged him not to slash any slopes when I'm not here.

Often in the evenings we'll stroll around the property, seeing everything differently now the bananas are gone. Sally wattles are turning up all over the place, and so too are Scotch thistles and fireweed. We'll have to get to those before they spread, but meanwhile we pluck as much of the fireweed as we can, stuffing the yellow flowers into jeans pockets to be burned off later. Fireweed is dangerous to cattle — that doesn't affect us personally but will impact on neighbours if it gets away.

Walking along the bottom of our northern slope that adjoins the national park, Christo pauses at a narrow path running through tall grass. 'Looks like a wallaby made a track. Want to see where it goes?'

'Sure. You go first.'

'What, in case there are snakes?'

'No, just, well, maybe … '

The path brings us out at a dam we didn't know existed. It's more or less in line with the two on Mark's property so it might be spring-fed, but it's much smaller and bounded by a barbed wire fence on the national park side. It must be on our land.

Native trees and ferns surround the dam and bulrushes grow on the far side. It's a scene crying out for a picnic basket, a cosy rug and a bottle of red wine. To think we've never seen this before.

Three months have passed since Bindi left us, and we've often talked about getting another dog, even another Airedale, but we usually come to the same decision. We don't want another dog, we want Bindi.

But fate intervenes. I ask Christo to take me to the Point and show me the results of the working bee's efforts on the concrete tank.

'What, you want to see the blood stains I left there?' Christo asks with a grin.

The volunteers have done a great job. Sea, sky and sand wrap around the big tank, concealing its ugly underbelly. Small craft sail on the river, seagulls wheel overhead and children play on the beach.

'Over the side,' says Christo, walking around the tank, 'is where I cut my knee open.' There is no blood.

We walk over to the Four Square and read the notices; most have been there for donkey's years but there's one new one.

Dizzy's pups. Pure-bred red kelpies. Free.

Amazing. Dizzy's pups. Greg's dog, Bindi's lovable former playmate. We haven't seen Greg or Dizzy for ages and certainly didn't know she was carrying.

'Look, Christo. Dizzy's pups. What if I ring Greg to see if he still has any left?'

'Well, if you like,' he agrees reluctantly.

Greg tells me he has one female, and she's ours if we want her, so we arrange to meet at the end of the day at his place. Just in case we decide to take her, I bring a small basket lined with a clean soft towel and pop in a soft toy. Also just in case, I toss a bottle of red on the back seat of the truck.

As soon as we walk down Greg's drive, four miniature Dizzys rush up to play at our feet, red-brown bundles of undiluted energy. I'm lost straight away.

Greg drives up behind us in a new ute, Dizzy beside him on the passenger seat.

'What do ya reckon?' he calls to us, laughing.

I catch Christo's eye. 'They are so beautiful, Greg.'

'Which one's the girl?' Christo is kneeling, fondling the tumbling puppies.

Greg lifts one of the two smallest and holds her to his chest. 'This one. See, she has Diz's white markings.'

With the back of his forefinger, he strokes the blaze of tufty white hair that runs from under her chin right down her chest.

'She's gorgeous. Can we have her?' My question is directed at Christo rather than Greg, who hands me the pup.

'It's up to you. If you like,' Christo says. For him, no dog will ever replace Bindi. But I have a good feeling about this little one.

'Have you given her a name, Greg?' The pup is already in my basket, curled into a sleepy ball.

'I've been calling her Loopy. She might end up being like Dizzy … a gorgeous dog but a handful. But call her what you like.'

'Are you sure you don't want money for her?' Christo asks.

'Nah. You're right.'

'Well, here's a bottle of red. A swap. Thanks a lot, mate.'

On the drive home, the puppy snuggles into the warmth of her hiding place.

'Loopy,' Christo says suddenly. 'Loopy … I like it. But not spelt like that, L-o-o-p-y. How about Lupi, Lupi Lou.'

'Mmmm … I dunno … yeah … Okay.'

And a tiny red kelpie enters our lives.

The festive season is going to be busy. Alix will be here for the customary two-day feasting and gift exchange, Alan and Kerrie are coming for New Year's and the Brisbane family will be here in between.

We pick up Alix at Coffs on Christmas Eve in time to call in at Nambucca, our favourite place for fresh seafood. It's a 30-minute drive from Grassy, but we make the effort because the fish is fresh, and the ambience is so special. Davis's seafood shop is a box-like room at the back of an ordinary house built right on the Nambucca River. A blackboard at their driveway lists what's for sale, but half the fun is going inside to see what they have on display.

The doorway guards against flies with a full-length curtain of colourful plastic strips. Customers squash up four abreast and two deep against the display counter. Seafood recipes from newspapers and magazines have been cut out and taped to the walls, the corners curling up.

'Have you tried the deep-sea bugs?' asks the bloke who runs the place, shelling one and distributing morsels to the customers.

'Let's get some for tonight, Dad,' Alix says. She's one of the lucky ones to sample the bugs. 'And what about some local prawns? I'll cook them with chilli and garlic and we'll have them with pasta.'

I add half a kilo of whiting fillets to the order. We'll have them on Boxing Day.

This is our third Christmas at Grassy Head and our little family moves comfortably into the established routine, with one last-minute crisis and one last-minute variation on tradition.

'Where's the Christmas tree?' Alix is horrified that we haven't put up any decorations one day out from Christmas, so I quickly remind her that I've been home for only a couple of days, and Christo has been busy watering, fertilising and slashing.

'Well, can we get one please? It won't be Christmas without a Christmas tree.'

Last Christmas Michael and Irene offered us one of the small pines that spring up like mad on their property and are regarded as an environmental pest. They've felled the big ones, replacing them with natives, but some small ones have survived. Michael is more than happy for us to take one.

Christo returns from their paddock with a fine specimen of *Pinus radiata* that fits perfectly into the nook that has become our Christmas tree spot.

Blue and silver is our colour scheme this Christmas. The cardboard star Alix handcrafted when she was little and plaited crêpe paper streamers we made together have, over the years, sunk to the bottom of the box of decorations to be superseded by shiny metallic balls and drizzles of tinsel.

So, crisis averted, dinner that night is a relaxed and happy affair as we feast on seafood.

The variation to the traditional menu has nothing to do with the sacrosanct turkey stuffing (I can see this recipe being handed down to Alix's kids one day), it's the dessert. Alix has requested a frozen chocolate log with raspberry coulis that I haven't made since we left Bondi Junction, and we construct it together, laughing and fighting over the cream-covered beaters.

Alix falls for little Lupi Lou and plays with her constantly. Which suits Lupi. She knows she was born to round up the herd, any herd, and she lies in wait to ambush Alix whenever she walks past, nipping at her heels to force her to travel in a particular direction and reducing Alix to giggles.

'She is so cute, Mum. I miss Bindi, but I love Lupi, too.'

And when the puppy tires, Alix cradles her on her lap, undoing all the progress we've made in teaching Lupi that she's to live outside. There go the polished parquetry floors.

Alix's visit comes to an end too quickly. On our drive back up to Coffs, I tell her that we're planning a big celebration for our anniversary in 2006.

'It's our twenty-fifth, and your father and I are going to renew our vows.'

'Really? That's so cool,' she says, pinning her long hair into a knot on top of her head. 'Up at Grassy?'

'Yes.'

'What are you going to do exactly?'

'Well, we haven't worked out any details yet, but it will involve eating and drinking and music. And lots of friends, we hope, though it's a long way for people to come.'

'Where will they all stay?'

'They can camp at our place in tents if they like, or stay at a caravan park or the Seventh-Day Adventist Convention Centre. We've got friends who run two B&Bs, as well.'

'Will you have a celebrant?'

'Hmmm … think so.'

'That is really, really cool … By the way,' Alix gives me her winning smile, 'I can have the guest room, huh? You wouldn't make me sleep in a tent.'

November isn't far away. We really must get cracking.

After Alix departs, we have one night on our own before the Brisbane tribe arrives; Mum is staying with Janet in Kempsey, my 'little' sister Kathleen and Mick with us.

It's not very often we three sisters get together, and I can't remember when all of us last spent Christmas with Mum.

Kathleen and Mick bowl up in his canopied ute, with Kathleen's long-haired chihuahua, Honey. The bossy little dog immediately starts trying to organise Lupi, which confuses the kelpie momentarily. Isn't she the one who does the rounding up? The two dogs run off at frenetic speed, chasing each other around the citrus trees, when our neighbours' new, enormous rottweiler/bull mastiff puppy Pepper turns up to join in the game. It's absolute bedlam, but at least Lupi isn't lonely.

Mick is great fun. His droll sense of humour and love of rock'n'roll make him an entertaining match for Christo. 'I see you're getting a lot of use out of your chook house, Gillian,' Mick comments dryly after inspecting the conversion he did on the still-empty shed.

Scratching at his bearded chin and giving me a sidelong glance, he adds: 'No excuse now for not having chooks.'

'Yeah, well, you'll have to ask her about that,' Christo joins in, pointing a thumb in my direction.

'You can't just walk into a shop and buy chooks, you know,' I retort, a little defensively. I do feel guilty because it's been a year since Mick built the chook house. 'It's taken me a while to find out where to get them. And I've been in Sydney so much I haven't had time to organise anything.'

'Yeah, yeah, whatever.' While Mick's sinking the boot in, Kathleen is training Lupi and Honey, who's three, to obey — with great results.

'Honey, come,' she commands, and little feet patter along the veranda for a treat. 'Lupi, come,' and the kelpie repeats the performance.

'But I know the name of a bloke who sells 'em now. Dave. He's at Bowraville. Told me to give him a ring after Christmas.'

Mick's grinning at me with both dimples. 'So. It's December 27. What's keeping you?'

'I thought Kathleen and I would go and get some one day … if you'd like to, Kath?'

'Sounds like fun. Yes, I'll come.'

I've borrowed a wire netting crate for the chooks from Janet who, being a rural mayor, naturally has such things in her possession. Kathleen and I head off for Bowra, which is 11 kilometres west of Macksville on a bitumen road that rolls along the Nambucca River and passes through verdant countryside where dairy and beef cattle graze in pastures alongside studs and pecan farms.

Bowra is an old town that thrived in the days before loggers finished off the last stands of native cedar and is now undergoing a revival triggered by its architectural charm. Homes and public buildings have been restored, as has the art deco theatre that now shows classic and cult movies and puts on plays.

Bowra has its troubled side, too, a history of shame that divides black and white people in the community. Three Aboriginal children were murdered there between October 1990 and January 1991 after parties on the outskirts of town at a subdivision known as The Mission; the person who killed them still hasn't been brought to justice. A local white man was charged with two of the murders and acquitted, but the unsolved crimes have spawned lingering hatred and distrust.

'The locals are working bloody hard to reconcile their community, though,' I tell Kathleen as we drive slowly down the main street, a wide picturesque avenue of quaint old shops and charming timber homes with deep awnings held up by wooden posts. They call it the veranda post town.

'The school has done a fabulous job and the community is really determined to solve all its issues, from the lack of law and order, which is a serious problem, and unemployment, which is also terrible. But those murders … '

On our way out of town, we pass a collection of brick houses on the left: The Mission. Many of the yards are overgrown. I wonder how you can mow the grass if you can't afford a mower. Unemployment here is very high.

We find Dave the chook man a few kilometres on the other side of town.

'Got 'em ready for you,' he says, three black-and-white dogs bouncing around the cage at his feet.

I asked him for six hens on the point of lay.

'You've got five New Hampshire Reds, they're the brown ones here,' he says, transferring them one by one into Janet's crate, 'and one Light Sussex. All good layers.' I don't know about the Hampshires but Dad used to have Light Sussex.

As Dave lifts out the white pullet, it flies from his grip into some shrubbery.

'Get him,' Dave calls to one of the excited dogs. The dog runs after, clamps its jaws firmly over the startled chook and then carries it gently back to Dave, apparently unharmed.

'Don't worry,' Dave says, turning to us. 'He didn't hurt the chook. But she's a bit shaken; I'll get you an Australorp.'

Six chooks, a bag of laying pellets, a bag of feed and some straw. Spanish omelet, here we come.

chapter fifteen

'It seems you can't have gracious living
and Goannas. Shiny villas multiply
On what were quite attractive bits of land
And we'll be getting sewerage by and by.'

'Outer Suburbs'
by John Manifold

Kathleen is concerned about Mum's health. Since she lives almost next door to Mum and sees her every couple of days, her opinion carries a lot of weight with Janet and me — if Kathleen's worried, we're worried.

'I'm concerned about two things. One is Mum's driving. I think she's getting worse. The other thing is that she's had a couple of falls.'

'Have you talked to her about all this?' Janet gets straight to the point.

'Well, no, I thought we should talk about it together first and decide what to do.'

Janet and I share another, but related concern. Mum is used to having Kathleen nearby. What if Kathleen wants to move away? And does Kathleen feel under pressure to stay for Mum's sake?

Now the three of us are together it's the perfect opportunity to talk about these things, although I feel uncomfortable discussing Mum behind her back.

I tell Kathleen that Janet and I have been talking about Mum coming to live down here at Stuarts Point.

Kathleen seems surprised at the idea, but it could be the solution to her concerns as well as ours.

A retirement home is out of the question; none of us could bear that. We're too close, mother-daughter friction apart.

In any case, Mum's already dealt with the issue. When she recovered from breast cancer she immediately went into planning mode. She filled out a living will to specify in a legally binding document her wishes in the event of serious illness ('I don't want you girls having to decide whether or not to turn off the life support if it gets to that stage. I'm making the decision now'), and then started inspecting Brisbane's retirement villages to find one she liked. In the event, she chose three and put her name down, asking them to check with her every six months.

'Moving here is a great idea.' Janet says.

Kathleen: 'I would miss her.'

'She could sell her house in Brisbane, buy one in Stuarts Point and have a bit left over,' I say, advancing my proposal further.

'Well, she might not have that much left over,' Kathleen warns. 'Remember the funny money.'

Last year Mum decided to take out an equity loan of $80,000 on her home and go travelling.

We all received the same text message: *Booking cheap flight US 2005. Will take first one who says yes. Muth xo*

Kathleen won the lucky dip, and Janet and I were quite happy to see her go with Mum. It was tempting, as Mum was shouting the fare and accommodation from the $80,000 'funny money' as she calls it, but neither of us could see our way clear to taking one month off.

Although they had a whale of a time, both came back convinced that Mum wasn't as physically — and possibly mentally — able at eighty as she had been at seventy.

It shouldn't have come as a surprise, but it did. And Mum was hit hard. She had plans to take Janet to Spain, me to the Kimberley, to share a month each with her. But the US experience had shaken her confidence.

Mum is going back to Brisbane with Kathleen and Mick, so we organise a family meeting the night before they depart to tell Mum what we've been discussing.

I wonder what she's feeling, sitting thoughtfully opposite her three offspring as they propose plans for her future. Yet with respect and dignity, she listens.

'Well, you have been busy working things out,' she says lightly.

Three pairs of eyes watch her anxiously.

'First, I want to tell you I'm touched that you all care so much about me. I know this is all about love. Second, regarding my driving, you're telling me I'm not safe on the roads?'

Three heads nod, guilty.

'You know I would be lost without my car?'

Again we nod. I feel somewhat ashamed, but we have agreed to stick together on this issue.

'Okay.' Mum takes a deep breath. 'How's this? When I get back to Brisbane, I will pay for a driving test. And if I pass,' she wags a finger at each of us in turn, 'you'll all have to eat humble pie.'

She makes us laugh.

'As for living down here, that's a big step. But I'll give it some serious thought.'

'Let's go down to the club while you're thinking,' I suggest. It's Tuesday, members' draw. Janet's off home and Kathleen and Mick want an early night.

Christo and I often go on Tuesdays, and now that we're regulars the mass of grey heads is no longer as amorphous. We see the same people sitting at the same tables in the same groups every week; some even smile back at us when we come in and sit down at our usual table.

We feel a definite sense of welcome, if not belonging, here and I'm sure Mum would enjoy the social life. Many members are keen bowlers, like her, and the club is just two blocks from the village shops.

The draw is supposed to be between 5.30 pm and 6.30 pm and, even though we're usually late, the first draw is never before 5.40 pm. We have plenty of time to order a drink.

'I'll have a claret, please,' Mum says to Christo, 'in a middy glass with ice, please.'

Hmmm. An interesting order. I go to the bar with Christo to get a cupful of free peanuts from the dispenser.

'Hungry? Here. Have some nuts, Mum.'

'Yes, thanks darling. What's the restaurant here like?'

'It's good country Chinese. I'm a sucker for the sweet-and-sour pork.'

She laughs. 'Bet it's not as good as mine.'

It's not, and I tell her so. When Dad worked for the insurance company, he threw a party at home once a year; he would cook curried prawns, she spent hours preparing sweet-and-sour, which she would serve in a scooped-out pineapple.

Suddenly I hear my number called for the $300 prize. The last time I won anything was almost thirty years ago in Vanuatu, during a Bastille Day dinner as guests of a local couple we knew; the evening was conducted in French, my number was called and I ran to the stage to collect my token for … $100 worth of building supplies. Our friends were most grateful.

It all comes back to me as I dig into my handbag for my purse to get out my membership card. No purse. Uh-oh.

Flustered, I skip up to Geoff, the bloke in charge of the club and the microphone. 'It's me, it's my number,' I whisper. 'But I forgot to bring my card.' I try out my version of Alix's winning smile on him.

'I'm sorry,' he shrugs apologetically. 'No card, no prize.'

Head down, I scuttle back to Christo. 'How embarrassing. You know what's worse? Technically I'm not even allowed to be in the club without my membership card. Um, I think I'd like to go.'

Mum polishes off her claret. 'You know, I like the feel of this place.'

The Bears come for New Year's, which we celebrate with more seafood and rosé than you could poke a stick at. Lupi has their dog Pax to play with, as well as Pepper from next door. It's an enchanted life for a puppy. But once Pax goes and she's on her own again, Lupi starts crying in her kennel outside our bedroom every night. Pepper usually visits at around 3 am for some reason so, even if we've finally fallen asleep listening to Lupi's sad whimpers, Pepper wakes us as he blunders across the veranda, knocking over pot plants with his long tail, to find his little mate.

'Christo, I've read somewhere that a working dog will cover up to 100 kilometres in a day. Maybe we should take her to the beach and she can run with you.'

'Worth a try,' he says, 'but you'll have to come too in case she won't follow me.'

We needn't have worried. As Christo launches into his jog along the sand, this staunch little pup — no bigger than a litre milk bottle — gallops along behind, having to take twice as many steps to keep up. Now I know where the word 'dogged' comes from.

Then I hear a yelp, and Christo is down.

'She ran between my legs,' he laughs between ragged breaths.

Rising to his feet, he picks her up and cups her face in his hand. 'You're really something.' She wriggles to get down, licks his hand with her pointed pink tongue and fixes him with her unblinking green eyes.

Getting Lupi was a good decision; every day we enjoy her more. She's a bowerbird, collecting all sorts of things and taking them into her kennel to hide under her blanket: plastic bottles, pieces of stick, and any shoes that are left outside. Tools vanish. A gardening glove. It becomes so crowded in there, it's a wonder she can find a soft spot for sleeping.

Lupi amuses us constantly, but before long we realise she needs the company of another dog, preferably a puppy. There are usually plenty of abandoned puppies after Christmas, and with that in mind I decide to contact the Macksville pound.

'Puppies. No, I don't have any puppies.' It's Reg, the bloke I spoke to when Bindi went missing.

'But I tell you what. I have the most beautiful dog in the world here, and he needs a home. As a matter of fact, I would keep him if I could, but I already have three dogs. He's a German koolie/collie cross, a very intelligent dog, and lovely to look at. Big patches of colour all over him, so I call him Pablo.'

'How old is he?'

'Not sure. About five, I think. I tell you what, he's one of the best dogs I've ever seen. Headstrong, though.'

'Is he aggressive?'

'No, he's been desexed and he has a lovely nature. He would never attack anyone. He does like to guard, though.'

'What's that mean?'

'He barks when people go past or come onto his territory.'

'I see.'

'Come over and have a look at him right now if you like. I'm here at the pound, down near the police station.'

We first spy Pablo from a distance, Reg walking him down the road towards the pound on a short lead.

'Wow. Will you look at that?' Christo says. He climbs out of the truck, obviously impressed.

Reg hands him the lead. 'Walk him a bit. See how you like him.'

Christo makes soothing noises to the big dog, and I can tell he's already decided. Then I notice Pablo's eyes are different colours: one bluey white, the other brown. It's a bit unsettling.

'Why don't you take him home for a couple of days and let me know how it goes. It's no problem if you don't want him.'

As soon as we get home, Christo loops a long rope through the handle of the lead so Pablo can move around on the veranda where we've assembled to reassure him (and Lupi) that all's well and he's welcome. Pablo stretches, flops to the floor at Christo's feet and falls asleep. Obviously the big dog thinks he's come to stay.

I keep calling him Pedro or Pancho by mistake, which makes it difficult to get his attention and in the midst of my confusion one day I stutter, 'Pedro … er Pancho… er Big Dog.' And Big Dog he becomes. Then all I have to do is remember to call him 'he'; Pablo is the first male animal we've owned.

Lupi and Pablo are getting on like a house on fire, Pablo showing infinite patience with the puppy, who is a constant nuisance. He's a magnificent dog, but he's teaching Lupi bad habits, chasing the truck whenever we drive off and running down to meet it on arrival. Pablo's big enough to be seen and is street wise, but Lupi isn't and one day Christo accidentally bumps her with the truck. With a startled yelp, Lupi hobbles onto the veranda; luckily she's not really hurt.

Pablo obviously needs some remedial work. He also creates havoc when we go down to the chook house, tearing around it and barking wildly. Somehow it doesn't appear to bother the hens, which cluck on regardless, but it annoys us, and no amount of shouting will stop him.

We decide to try a new tactic before Lupi copies this behaviour too. Walking down with both dogs, we call Pablo (who ignores us and begins racing around and barking) and then Lupi (who always comes). Lupi is patted and fussed over while Pablo is ignored. After three days, it's having an effect and after a week Pablo has given up impressing us with his rodeo tactics. If only we had half a dozen cattle or sheep for these two.

It's difficult to believe that only one year has passed since we planted two hundred and fifty tube stock at the bottom dam.

The eucalypts have soared to twice our height, along with the red and white cedars, which have been attacked by tip moths, making them bushy and unsuitable for cutting, but they look wonderful anyway. *Leptospermums* weep graciously to the ground beside the dense purplish foliage of *Syzygium australe*.

I've run out of red marker dye, but I don't really need it. Except for a delicate shade-loving groundcover I haven't been able to identify, the weeds are concentrated in open spaces or around slow-growing species that haven't yet formed enough cover to shade out the interlopers. It's a simple matter to spray the isolated patches of weeds, mostly the good old cobbler's pegs, noogoora burr and clover.

The tobacco bush is prolific but easy to pull out by hand when it's small, and lantana has given up altogether. On the dam side of the wallaby fence, Christo can just squeeze in one pass with the tractor.

We've lost a few plants, maybe ten; perhaps our place didn't suit them. But native violets are springing up all over the forest and, since we started keeping the weeds down, the self-seeded tree ferns and lilly pillies growing on the banks of the dam have really taken off. Other natives have found a home here too, courtesy of the birds, which we can hear chattering and singing above our little creek. It's been running again after the summer's rains, though only just; if I stop and concentrate I can hear it gurgling quietly.

On the other side of the creek, we've had a large section of lantana cleared. It's now in a big pile we'll burn in winter, although Jim says there's no need: it will mulch down and provide shelter for the wildlife in the meantime. I hope he doesn't mean snakes.

Jim and Margaret have grubbed out most of their lantana by hand over the years but we decided to take a shortcut because the enormity of the task was so daunting and our tractor would never have handled the slippery conditions; there's still plenty left for us to do.

Jack, who slashed for us, uncovered an old track that gives us better access to the lantana between the track and the creek. Now we can see from one side of the dam to the other and I feel we're progressing.

Big Dog has claimed the dam as his private swimming hole. Reg, from the pound, told us Pablo loved the beach and we saw how true that was the first time we took him to the leash-free part of Grassy when he barrelled into the surf, hurdling the waves and warning off a flotilla of seagulls as an incredulous Lupi looked on.

At the dam, he dives in and swims laps, puffing and grunting as if he's about to drown. Lupi doesn't particularly like the water; she'd rather be on safe ground.

Watching these two lovely dogs at play in this beautiful place evokes memories of Bindi; the dogs have given us so much joy. Looking up at a clear blue sky through the broad-spreading branches of a red cedar, my mind wanders off on a tangent. What would it have been like if we'd had more children? Loving Alix so much, could I feel the same way about a second, third or fourth child? We didn't get the chance to find out, but I'm sure I know the answer.

'Let's have a party in January to celebrate the rainforest turning one, and invite everyone who helped us get it going. Margaret and Jim, Damon and Sharon, Michael and Irene, Dave and Pam, Robbo and Jane, the two Gregs, the Wilsons … ' I suddenly realise how many people we have come to know and like, in a relatively short time.

'Okay.' Christo's enthused. 'What do you reckon? Barbecue a leg of lamb, a leg of pork, and get some sausages?'

Our guests insist on bringing salads and nibbles and desserts, the gourmet food of friends, and it's a night of feasting and fun. We have truly arrived.

The chooks show no inclination to leave the chook house after a week of being locked in, a suggestion Mick made so they would become used to their new environment. They huddle under the shelf of nesting boxes Christo made from used plastic fertiliser containers, grumbling to each other and sticking so close together I can never be sure they're all there.

Every morning I check each of the six straw-lined boxes for eggs, in vain, and visit again in the late afternoon to freshen up their water and shut them in to keep foxes out. Although the overhanging branches of a nearby mango tree help keep the pen cool, the western sun is so low that there's almost no shade for them inside, so I attach a double thickness of shade cloth over half the front.

They still huddle and grumble when I go down there, but at least I feel better. We gave up eating battery and cage eggs long ago; I reckon chooks deserve better than that.

One morning I open up to find one of the beautiful New Hampshire Reds dead on the dirt floor, right in the middle, her sisters squashed into the usual spot.

I can't see a mark on her, but she's dead all right. Christo puts her in a plastic bag and dumps the carcase in the bin. What can have killed her? A disease of some kind? They all look extremely healthy to me. Oh, well.

The next day I hear a loud cackling from the chook house, like the noise they make when they're laying, but more strident, more urgent.

'Christo, quick, something's happening down at the chook house,' I yell, shoving my feet into my gardening clogs and scuttling as fast as I can over the uneven ground. Inside the chook house a New Hampshire Red and the Australorp lie dead, their bodies torn and bloody.

The remaining chooks are setting up a helluva racket on top of the nesting boxes.

A fox? Hang on, the door was shut and nothing has breached the chicken wire. How … ?

Under the shelf of nesting boxes, blending in with the grey tin walls, is a lace monitor that is easily 2 metres long.

Standing in the doorway, tears of anger and sadness streaking my cheeks, I scream at the goanna and start throwing rocks at it. 'Get out. Get out!'

'Honey, I think you should come away. That thing could tear you to bits.'

Christo pulls me away and I hide my face from the sight of the two dead hens as he approaches the lace monitor from behind, urging it to escape through the now empty doorway.

'It must have come onto the roof from the mango tree, then crawled in through this gap between the roof and the wall. The chooks didn't have a chance.' He comes over to where I'm sitting on the ground. 'Are you okay, babe?'

'Yes. I'll be all right. Poor bloody chooks.'

What a disaster. That afternoon, Christo cuts away all the overhanging branches. We capture the three traumatised survivors and take them in the back of the truck up to the greenhouse, where they will be safe until we can block the openings.

It doesn't take long to make the chook house goanna-proof, or at least we hope the rolled-up chicken wire we tack in place will do the job. Getting the chooks out of the igloo is going to be much more difficult.

For a start, it's raining and they've managed to leave droppings all over the cement floor. It might just be a bit slippery.

There are steel mesh potting benches around three sides and another in the middle, creating two walkways that are essentially dead ends.

Slowly I approach the nervous group of hens in the corner, clucking to them. 'Boo-ook … boo-ook, boo-ook.' I really make pretty good chook noises, I reckon.

Down on my knees I go, reaching under the bench with both hands and … Squawk. All three have scattered, knocking over orchids and spilling soil everywhere.

Christo lunges for one near him and gets purchase on more than feathers.

I peer at him, rain splattering on my face. 'Well done, darling.'

He shuts the door behind him and deposits the hen in the truck.

I am now crawling down one of the paths, aiming for another cackling quarry. She sidesteps to the other path. I crawl over the concrete and feel something squish under my knee. My prey is still, I lunge, she flies to safety. Christo makes for her and scares both hens into flight and a deafening cacophony. They're not having a good week, apparently.

I steal up to my nervy prey, now backed into a corner under the bench. 'Boo-ook, boo-ook,' I say in my chook voice. She turns her head sideways to cock an eye at me, feathers trembling in readiness for flight. I recall Dave the chook man asking me if I wanted their wings clipped. But no, I wanted them to be free and live as naturally as possible.

In desperation I lurch at her, hands clutching nothing but air, and she flies into Christo's arms.

'You know what, darling,' I say from my watery seat, 'I think we'll leave the last one here until later.'

Eventually all three hens are back in their pen, safe from marauders, but before the week's out one has disappeared and another has died — apparently from natural causes (or fright after the ordeal) — and one hen remains. I call her Rita.

Irene's giving salsa lessons at the community hall, and Christo's agreed to come with me to try it out. The acoustics are terrible and it's difficult to hear Irene, so I concentrate on her feet to guide me through the twisting rhythm. I find it's a bit like aerobics — miss one step and you lose the lot. Carl, who agists the Clydesdales and ponies in the paddock down the hill from us, is much in demand as a partner. It's not just that he's the only other man, he dances as if he were born to it, back straight, shoulder-length blond hair swinging and his feet confidently marking out the moves.

We practise at home: one-two, one-two-three. My thighs ache with the hip-swaying effort, but I don't ever get it right.

Irene's salsa classes are part of the rebirth of the hall, as Greg the newsagent had hoped. With money raised by the senior citizens and contributions from the council, it's being extended and the stairs and fence repaired. As every week passes, there's more progress. Soon there's to be landscaping work done by volunteers.

The library, where school kids get the opportunity to work on computers, has extended its hours to be open two afternoons a week.

During the SPADCO annual general meeting, at which I'm re-elected to the committee, there's news of more improvements to the village as the council has allocated $80,000 to 'road-related' projects. We could get boring old kerbing and guttering or something more exciting — cycleways, footpaths or beautification of the main street. My role in all this is to work on a questionnaire to get feedback from the community.

Next up, Kevin reports on the progress of the draft management plan committee and, while I'm not on that subcommittee, I'm passionate about the issue of the future development of the district. Our community has the chance to submit our vision to the state government, have it legislated, so that Yarrahapinni, Stuarts Point and Grassy Head go forward in ways that celebrate and support diversity of culture, environment, history and specialties.

The last item on the AGM agenda is the announcement that council will be replacing the footbridge because it's not safe.

The news makes me gasp. 'The footbridge? You can't tear down the footbridge.' All eyes have turned to me.

'It's a part of our history, it makes Stuarts Point special.' I'm as surprised as the crowd at my outburst.

'Yeah. Too right.' A young man behind me smiles.

'But it's not safe,' my SPADCO colleague Glenda, who's sitting beside me, says. She looks a bit cross with me. 'We can't have anyone being hurt on that silly old bridge.'

I can't imagine the Point without its crooked white bridge. It's been sketched, painted, photographed, even written about in a children's book.

'I don't know what you're on about,' Ian T calls out from the back of the hall. 'The bridge is only forty years old, it's nothing special. The bridge that was there when I was a kid was much better. At high tide the middle of the bridge was under water, and it was great fun.' This brings a bout of laughter from everyone, me included.

I take a mental step back.

'Well, maybe, but you know we can't just let things that are unique to our village disappear or fall into ruin. There are important historic sites around here, like the midden at the Golden Hole … '

Someone interrupts, curious. 'Midden? I didn't know there was a midden … '

'And the pilot's station at Grassy … '

'Where's that?'

'Even the old 1932 post office is still here. We should be identifying things like this and making sure we don't lose them.'

'And the stories of the old-timers,' Sue adds. 'And old photographs. They need to be looked after.'

Nicky, who has the floor, is laughing. 'Well, you've caused quite a stir, Gillian. Maybe we should go back to the council and find out more about the footbridge.'

Greg nods. 'Gillian, since all this is so important to you, I think you should head up a history subcommittee.' There's a buzz of agreement and after the meeting I'm overwhelmed with ideas and questions.

Bingo. I've become a historian.

Here we go. Another blackout and it's Saturday afternoon. Well, I suppose we can read the papers, or do the cryptic crossword. Power should come back on soon. If not, the Mid Coast Glamour Girls (a regional drag show) won't be thrilling the punters at the tavern tonight — unless they have a generator.

'I'll give Country Energy a call,' Christo announces, abandoning the cryptic in the failing light, 'see what their recorded message has to say.' The number for Country Energy's hotline is imprinted on his brain, the only phone number he knows by heart.

'It's the Rocks, Stuarts Point, Grassy Head and Middle Head. They're working on it.'

The candles live in the kitchen bench because we need them so often, and Christo maintains the batteries in our two torches in case of such emergencies. And we have the battery-operated radio. And a cask of drinkable red. We're fine for now.

By 7 pm, I'm hungry.

'I reckon it's peanut butter sandwiches tonight, love.'

'That'll do me. I'll check the power company while you're preparing dinner by torchlight. Very romantic.'

I get a hug as he walks past.

The recorded message says the power will be back around midnight, and we hold out as long as we can but, even with the red to take the edge off our boredom, we're yawning by 9.30 pm.

Frustrated, I push the newspaper away from me. 'I can't do any more of this sudoku by candlelight or I'll go blind, like John Donne.'

'I think it takes more than one night, babe, and he did turn out a fair bit of poetry.'

'Whatever … darling, I've been thinking.'

'Er, yes.' Christo laughs, abandoning the cryptic.

'I've been thinking that I'd like to have some sort of memorial for your parents, here at Grassy Head.'

'Like what?'

'Well, I don't know, something, something better than they got, something that says they mattered. They don't have a rose or a plaque or anything.'

'I hardly knew my parents, babe, I hardly remember them.'

'That sort of makes it more important they're not forgotten. You're the last of the family … well, the last male … '

Christo's elder brother Gerry died while we were in New Zealand.

'It would be good to celebrate their lives. They suffered a helluva lot in their lifetime and now it's as if they never existed. I would like, in some way, to pay tribute to your parents.'

Christo drains his wine glass. Have I intruded too far? I can't read his face in the dim light.

'What did you have in mind?'

I've thought about this a lot. 'A tree. I'd like us to plant a tree for them, a shady tree on the hill overlooking Grassy.'

'Let me think about it.' He refills my glass and then his, and we sit silently in the flickering candlelight.

There's little Christo remembers of his parents: Arthur and May both died before he turned thirteen. May Taylor was a rosy-cheeked nineteen when she married the dashing Arthur Nicholson, a clerk four years her senior. They were both natives of Manchester in England but marrying Arthur was a move up in the world for May; she was a factory worker.

A son, Gerry, was their first-born, then there was a daughter who died when she was very young. Arthur returned home from the war a hero and in 1947, eighteen years after Gerry's birth, the couple had another son. They called him Christopher.

For the sake of the family's future, Arthur decided they would leave the factory smog of Manchester behind and they emigrated to Australia in 1950, settling in Newborough East, a workers' estate on the brown coalfields east of Melbourne.

But May, so far away from everything and everyone she knew, suffered a breakdown. Her future was to unravel behind bars in 'mental' institutions in Sunbury, Victoria and Toowoomba, Queensland where she received electric shock treatments — and no hope.

Arthur, who had gamely done his best to raise his boy alone and hold down his job with the State Electricity Commission, who had survived Dunkirk and the African campaign as a despatch rider, died of a heart attack at the age of fifty-two. May died three years later, of pneumonia.

Their ashes were scattered in a Melbourne cemetery. No marker notes their passing.

'Planting a tree for them is a nice idea,' Christo says softly.

chapter sixteen

'Dance like there's nobody watching
Love like you'll never get hurt
Sing like there's nobody listening
Live like it's heaven on earth
And speak from the heart to be heard.'

William W. Purkey

'Do you think it's silly to be renewing our vows? Some of our friends think it's weird.' I've tracked Christo down in the garage, where he's topping up the tractor with diesel. Our shiny green tractor has lost its shine: scratches on the bonnet, mud caked in the tyres, a big tear in the yellow seat patched with black gaffer tape. Now it looks like a real farm vehicle.

'Of course not. What brought that on?' He screws the cap back onto the jerry can, slides it away under the bench and wipes his greasy hands on his jeans.

'I've been thinking.'

I get the eyebrow lift. 'Uh-huh,' he says, squatting down to examine the tractor tyres to see if they need air as he waits for me to continue.

'We can't really renew our vows. I mean, what we promised back then, well, it's different now because … '

'Because we're old?' Christo grins up at me as he moves to the next tyre. 'We're too old to be in love?'

'Well, no, but … I don't know. What are we going to do? Are we going to get someone to officiate? It's not legal or anything, so how will it work? Maybe we should go to Italy for our anniversary instead. We've never been to Italy.'

'Are you getting cold feet? Hey, you're the one who proposed to me, remember? No, I like the idea of a party.'

Christo stands and leans back on the tractor, arms crossed in his deep-in-thought pose.

'Gillian, you are the best thing that ever happened to me. You and Alix.' He walks over to me and lifts my chin so he is staring straight into my eyes.

'I love you and I'm proud that you love me. I want the world to know it.'

He can still make me feel like a coy schoolgirl. Overwhelmed, I wrest my eyes away from his steady gaze, but he pulls me firmly into his gentle arms.

'It's going to be a wonderful party.'

'Yeah … I know.'

'So what's bothering you?'

'I dunno. It's just that we haven't done any major planning, I suppose.'

'Well, I love your idea of a gourmet barbecue. That doesn't need much planning. We'll get a couple of legs of lamb from Dangerous Dan, maybe some pork …'

'Well, if you're happy with that, I am.'

'I'm more than happy with that, love, and it's easy.'

'What will we get to drink?'

'Lots of bubbles, a dozen sauvignon blanc, beers …'

'And a case of shiraz,' I add. Christo does like a nice red.

'And we could hire a band,' he says enthusiastically. 'Someone local … '

'Except we don't know anyone local.'

'Well, we'll just have to start going out and listening to pub bands every weekend until we find one we like.'

Sounds great. We have to put on a good show.

He moves across to the compressor and turns it on.

'Let's do some solid planning tonight, huh? I want to finish slashing the section over near the fence before lunch. Okay?'

'Sure.'

As he climbs onto the tractor and fires it up, Big Dog barks furiously and starts running around the garage. Lupi, with her wild green kelpie eyes, watches intently as if debating whether to join him, but doesn't. She's a bit too small to go darting around tractors.

'Do you think we should ask Janet to officiate, or whatever?' I yell at Christo over the noise.

'Honey, from what I've seen of Janet's mayoral clobber, she wouldn't thank us for having to wear it in the heat of November,' Christo replies with a laugh. 'Besides, she'll be a guest. We'll work something out.'

'That's another thing, the guest list. Who are we going to invite?'

'Well, those who were at our wedding — those who are still alive — and new friends.'

'What will we say on the invitation?'

'Leave it to me.'

Here's Mum, blowing her horn as she comes up the drive, come to stay in Stuarts Point for three months to see if she could live here permanently. I want so much for it to work. One of the most difficult things to achieve in life is a normal relationship with your mother, and Mum and I have had our fair share of tensions. But now I feel there's a real chance we'll become friends.

'I'm only staying with you for two nights,' she announces, tugging at an overnight bag that's wedged between her most precious possessions — her computer and her television — in the back of the station wagon.

'However I would appreciate your help moving into my unit, and after that I'll be independent.'

She looks tired, but then she's been working hard for the past three or four weeks, using this visit as an excuse to get rid of clutter in her Brisbane house. I grab her bag, and match her shuffling pace up the ramp to the house.

'By the way, Gilly, I paid for a driving test and the instructor says I'm safer on the road than a lot of people half my age.' Mum will be eighty-two in June. Humble pie it is then!

She slips into the way of life at Stuarts Point instantly. Before the week is out, she's become a member of the Workers' Club and signs up for indoor bowls and the fishing club.

Wednesday afternoon is her first bowls day and, as I drive by on my way to the shop, I notice her car is outside.

It's right on 5 pm. What's she doing here so late? On my way back the car's still there. I can't resist going in to see what's happening. Bowls must have finished a couple of hours ago.

I spy Mum deeply engrossed in conversation with three other women, none of whom I know.

'Hello, darling.' She greets me with a big smile and hand outstretched, pulling me to her table. 'Come and meet the bowling girls.'

There's Hazel and Heather and Trish and … I'm not sure who is who, but they smile and ask me to sit down. 'So, you're the Grassy Head daughter,' one says. 'Your mother has told us all about you, and that she's the mayor's mother.'

I'm dumbfounded. She's made friends already.

'Would you like a drink, darling?' Mum asks.

'Well, just one, but I'll buy. What will you have?'

'Just ask for a Norma Special, love, they know what that is.' Here less than a week and she has her own order at the bar. The staff don't even know my name!

The Norma Special is a wine glass of claret poured into a tumbler — with ice in summer, without ice in winter. Guess it's quicker to say a Norma Special than all that and, if you're Norma and they see you coming, it's ready before you can say Jack Robinson.

A week after Mum's arrival, Mick drives down from Brisbane in a ute packed with big items she couldn't fit into her car — and Kathleen's dog Honey, to keep her company. It's the beginning of a love affair, and an exercise program for both of them. Honey needs daily walks.

Mum's three months in Stuarts Point are marvellous fun for me: running into her at the newsagency, meeting up with her on Tuesdays for the members' draw, having her for dinner, popping into her place for coffee. We haven't lived together for forty years, not even in the same town; we have decades of catching up to do.

Mum taps into aspects of Stuarts Point that are totally new to me: the mini-bus with a covered trailer (for shopping bags) that takes people into Kempsey once a fortnight; the 'permanents' from the holiday park and the 'part-timers' who spend six months here every year before returning to their homes elsewhere; her advisers at the hardware store, Pud and Arch.

My heart gives a happy leap whenever I bump into her unexpectedly down at the Point. One day I see her car outside the community hall and tiptoe up to the door and sneak a peek; she's playing indoor bowls, laughing with her new friends.

On Anzac Day, under perfect blue skies, Christo and I go down to the club to watch the procession. Leading the march is a bloke in a mobility scooter; behind him are the veterans, school kids in uniform, war widows, officials in suits and dads with toddlers on their shoulders. All keep respectful time to the music blaring from a speaker in the back of a station wagon that travels at a snail's pace out in front.

Suddenly I notice Mum on the other side of Ocean Avenue, Honey on a long lead. Mum looks so pretty, a strange thing to say about an eighty-two-year-old, but it's true. She's wearing a pink straw hat and a pink blouse, and they flatter her pale skin. She's fitter than when she arrived, and has lost weight.

Maybe she's loving it here, maybe she'll stay for good.

We listen to the Anzac Day speeches, then head to the club for an RSL Club fundraiser, a jumble sale. Mum carries Honey inside in a basket, to the delight of all her friends and the stern glances of the officials.

Her time at Stuarts Point goes quickly, too quickly. One marvellous day she and I go fishing from a gated jetty at Fisherman's Reach. She's somehow met and made friends with the jetty's owners, who have told her of the key's secret hiding place so she can fish there whenever she likes. As afternoon flows into evening, we share the silent pleasure of our companionship and the thrill of seeing a dolphin splashing in the shallows beneath our feet. It's an experience I will treasure for ever.

She's leaving in two weeks. 'Mum would you like to come with us to the Fredo pub on Sunday? There's a new blues club starting up there and we thought we might pop over for a look. If we like them, we might hire them for our wedding anniversary.

'Why, I'd love to.'

We park around the back of the pub, stopping for a minute to stare out across the wide Macleay and its grassy banks. Inland the drought has taken grim hold, but we've been lucky.

'It's so peaceful here,' Mum says wistfully. I think of her working-class cottage in Brisbane, two streets back from the never-ending roar of busy Kessels Road.

From the pub, the strains of a hot blues harp call us out of the wind and cold and we pull open the door to find the band in full swing, a band of old blokes.

The grin on Christo's face is a classic. 'They're old farts like me,' he says, heading for the bar. 'And they're not bloody bad.'

Mum and I grab three bar stools and dig the band: the bald blues harp player in tracky daks and thongs, lead guitarist all 'neat casual' wearing pristine runners, the salt-and-pepper bearded bass player (obviously a ZZ Top fan) and the drummer, an earnest fellow with a trimmer beard.

Unfortunately they're almost finished the set, but there are more top musos to come — and more great music.

I turn to Mum after a while and see she's dabbing her eyes.

'What's wrong? Are you okay?'

She nods and smiles, but tears streak her face. 'I'm just having such a wonderful time. I don't want to go home.'

Taking her hand and squeezing it, I have to turn away. Big girls don't cry.

Rita has begun laying, and everything about it is wrong. It's almost winter for a start, when chooks rarely lay or at least slow down their production, but Rita has chosen the shortest day of the year to present us with an egg. Three eggs, actually. We were away for a couple of days and when we return, three perfect white eggs are lying in one of the straw-lined nesting boxes.

Not only is it the wrong time of year, we haven't been giving her laying pellets because we've run out, so she's been getting the standard mix of corn, mash and molasses in her feed dispenser. Something is definitely odd about Rita, but it's not her eggs; the yolks are a vivid yellow and when I poach them for brekkie the whites stay intact instead of shredding into strings the way store-bought eggs do. And the flavour is wonderful.

'Well, blow me down and call me Shorty,' my sister the mayor says when I ring to tell her, employing her favourite expression of surprise. Janet is our authority on chooks.

'How long since she's had any pellets?'

'Oh, about two months, I think.' We didn't really take much notice since she wasn't laying anyway, and excused her from duty on the basis of having survived the lace monitor and the attentions of Big Dog.

'And you got the chooks after Christmas, on the point of lay, didn't you?'

'Yeah, that's right.'

'Well, keep her going. What you want to do is buy a china egg from the produce store and leave it in her favourite nesting box to encourage her to lay there. And get some more laying pellets. I can't believe it.'

'Do you think maybe she's been laying somewhere else?' Rita free-ranges for most of the day.

'That's a good point. She might have a nest outside and when you went away she couldn't get out so she laid in the chook house. How funny.'

We're just delighted to have these beautiful eggs, and one a day is plenty for the two of us. Still, the supply isn't constant and it seems we will either have to regulate her free-range hours or find her stash.

Rita's a nice friendly chook and not easily thrown into a panic, so I follow her when I let her out one morning. She pecks her way out of the chook house, stopping to enjoy an insect or two under the infamous mango tree, home of the goanna, then struts off down the track, never glancing back. I hang behind stealthily, taking cover behind the cow cane as she pokes around sheltered spots I think I would choose as nests if I were a hen. But after fifteen minutes I'm feeling like a bit of a duffer and give up; after all, Christo might be watching.

Rita obviously has struck a secret protection deal with the lace monitor to supply it with eggs.

We have another animal mystery on our hands: one of the dogs is killing rats and mice. Twice in the morning we find dead mice on our veranda, not a pretty sight, but one day I almost tread on a huge dead rat at the bottom of the stairs.

My stomach churns while Christo admires its size before taking it to the bin, dogs trotting along behind. Our mystery hunter delivers a smaller rat the very next day and dead mice keep turning up on the veranda for a couple of weeks. We can't pick which dog is the ratter but I suspect it's Pablo, who's always chasing after birds and little lizards. Not that I've seen him catch anything.

'It's Lupi,' Christo tells me confidently. That's Janet's guess too because, she says, kelpies are so quick.

'No, it must be Pablo.'

Christo has an amused glint in his eye. I smell, um, a rat.

'So-o-o … what makes you so certain?'

'I chained Pablo up last night because he wouldn't stop barking, and there's the proof.' He points to another large rat on the ground, well out of Pablo's reach.

'Well, little Lupi Lou, you've earned your keep. Just make sure you stick to rats and mice, huh. We don't want you hunting the native wildlife.'

Time we built a fence around the house.

Mum is leaving, her car once again stashed full of boxes, the computer and the television. Everything she couldn't fit in the car is in the packing shed: her futon bed, a washing machine, shelving, chairs, a shopping trolley, plastic containers and labelled cartons.

'I've had a wonderful time,' she says, getting into the car. And she looks it. She's full of life, lightly tanned and has lost almost 6 kilograms.

'See you in November for the party. Don't let the rats get into my things.'

It feels odd without Mum. To see her virtually every day and then not at all. She hasn't decided whether she'll come to live here but she's left a lot of stuff behind, including her precious fishing gear. And while that remains in the packing shed, I reckon she is counting on being back soon — for good.

It's a sublime winter's afternoon. On days such as this when Janet and I were little, Mum would take us to Southport on the train and she'd paint as we played on the beach. She looked so beautiful with bright red lipstick and a scarf tying back her wavy hair as she squirted oil paints onto her palette from small silver tubes.

She was never like any other mothers I met; she believed she could change the world. A peace activist, in 1967 she tried to deliver a letter of protest to South Vietnam's Air Vice Marshall Ky, who was visiting Brisbane. The security police threw her to the ground and held her down while they kicked her. They broke her foot.

Ten years later, aged fifty-seven, she was grinning with excitement in the grounds of Brisbane's Griffith University, waving a piece of paper certifying that she had just graduated with an Arts degree; my mother, who left school at fourteen. But this degree wasn't the end; it was the beginning of an academic career, the impetus for writing a textbook, *Industrial Relations in Japan: The Peripheral Workforce*, a return to painting after thirty-odd years, a degree in Fine Arts.

She was with me in 1984 when Alix was born, and I felt the awesome connection of three generations. No way would I let the rats get to her furniture.

Sally wattles are reclaiming the slope where bananas once grew, now showing their glorious winter mantle of yellow. On the high side of our drive is a tree fern valiantly striking up through a clump of lantana.

Bloody lantana. We must get rid of it on the other side of the creek so we can plant more rainforest. With a bit of luck, we might even be able to have it done before our anniversary. Palms and cycads would work well there, and native ginger; it's flourishing in the shade on the far bank.

Perhaps there'll be time to plant the avenue of silky oaks, too. They're glorious this year, leaves turning mustard yellow for winter. I expect by the time we celebrate our thirtieth wedding anniversary they'll be 5 or 6 metres high.

But, I'm dreaming again. There's no chance we'd get the wallaby fence up and the spraying done in time to plant the avenue of silky oaks, too: *Grevillea robusta*.

Beyond the packing shed a crescent moon rises white against the pale blue sky. My eyes wander towards the ocean, scanning for container ships at the edge of the world, but for now the horizon is empty. Two yachts tack into the westerlies and fishing boats cluster off Grassy Head. A hawk hovers over Frog Hollow waiting for its prey to break cover.

I shade my eyes with my hands and search vainly for whales. We've missed the famed white whale that passes every year; it's already been spotted up north at Byron Bay. Perhaps we'll catch sight of it on its return to the Antarctic in spring.

Our lives are more in tune with the seasons now, the heady anarchy of our early days at Grassy long gone. I rarely go to Sydney. Christo and I work together on the *recipes+* magazine and, when the weather allows, tend to the rainforest and our vegie garden.

The packing shed has become my escape, though I'm not sure that I have anything to escape from; it's more an escape to something. To no phone, no electricity, no interruptions. I bring my laptop down here and write, sitting at a wooden table that Mum picked up at a Stuarts Point garage sale for $10.

The table is flush up against a massive doorway that's a good 2 metres above the ground. I imagine the Pavans brothers, the original banana farmers here, backing a truck up to it and loading their cartons of ripening fruit into the back.

Once the equally massive door of timber-framed tin slides away, the light pours in. Framed by the doorway, the view is like a colossal pastoral painting. It's a work in progress: eucalypts shedding their stiff brown bark, swifts and swallows swooping on insects, a flurry of dust swirling across the curve of our road.

Pablo and Lupi come with me most days. After sniffing inside and out for rats and snakes, they flop down to snooze in rivers of sun streaming onto the floor through windows that have no glass.

And so I sit wrapped in the past of our banana farm, enclosed by rough plank walls that allow sea breezes to enter through timeworn gaps. I found a big old weighing scale (imperial measures) under the packing shed and stood it behind me against the wall; beside it is another found treasure, a sword-like gouging tool that was used to cut out the soft hearts of unwanted banana suckers. Two rusty roller belts that once bore the weight of banana cartons as they slid along have become benches, supported underneath by a row of empty weedkiller containers.

There are no bananas to be seen on the slopes now, although we've kept thirty or so below the home orchard, more than enough for me and our visitors. I don't think this property will ever go under bananas again. Ironically, the devastation wrought in north Queensland by Cyclone Larry last February came just as the last bananas withered away. The crop could have been worth tens of thousands of dollars. But life here isn't about the money.

We haven't become farmers, but we tend our passions and our health and our ethics here. These are the things I write about in the banana packing shed as I look over our well-travelled road.

I still learn things every day, and every day I am more reassured that moving to Grassy was the right decision. The signs that I'm right are all around me: magpies filling the air with sweet flute-like music; our rainforest towering high above the dam where I still dream of holding weddings; a husband who sings as he drives off in the tractor; my happy heart.

epilogue

Spring, and the winds howl in from all directions. Hot flashes arrive from the west; southerly busters bring gusty, cool change. Nor-easters whip up towering breakers. Branches snap from giant wattles; thank goodness for the chainie.

I wouldn't mind the wind except that we're trying to get the place ready for our anniversary, planting grevilleas and lilly pillies in newly made gardens. Christo creates boulder sculptures, cleans the veranda, dislodges mud-wasp nests. I taste-test elaborate Middle Eastern recipes I'm planning for our forty guests.

Mum's an early starter, here to help us and see her friends at the Point. It's Sunday, a big night — members' draw and the meat raffle. Down the club we go to meet her.

From our table we see Mum coming towards us, being greeted with hugs from old mates on the way. She collapses into a chair beside me as Christo goes to the bar for a Norma special. Her eyes are dancing. 'What a welcome! I'm playing bowls on Wednesday and some of the girls are organising a morning tea.'

'Sooo ... don't keep me in suspense. Have you made a decision about moving?'

'Well,' she sips her claret, 'yes. I'm going to look into the market when I get home, and if I can get a good price for my house ... I'll come here to live.'

Blinking in surprised delight, it takes me a minute to realise her number has been called in the meat raffle.

Party day. Up to Nambucca for bread rolls and prawns, and Macksville to Dangerous Dan's for sausages. We've run out of chocolate and hazelnut yogurt for the frozen desserts.

Suddenly, another last-minute thought. 'Christo, you know what we haven't done?'

'What?'

'Written what we're going to say.'

'Hmmm … why don't we reaffirm what we said last time. You said you'd obey, didn't you?'

Cheeky bugger.

'And we should say something about looking forward to another twenty-five years … '

Alix takes over the desserts. Mum and Mick are decorating the tables, fighting the gathering wind. Janet's in the kitchen making salads. I'm finishing off a giant chickpea salad.

'Chickpeas. Lovely,' Alix says dryly.

'Oh. Don't people like chickpeas?'

'Mum, I was just teasing.'

'Janet, do you like chickpeas?'

'I couldn't say they're my favourite.'

Rosie has arrived, bearing a bunch of white carnations. I know she doesn't like chickpeas. 'Don't worry,' she says. 'Some people love them.'

Groan.

June's here. From Bathurst. With a sensational magnolia.

'My dear, I love chickpeas. Can I help?'

Then Jenny arrives from Brisbane; I put all hands onto prawn peeling while I splash more balsamic onto my salad.

Now who's here? Right. The blues band, PP Hardigan and the Blues Nuts.

I have to write those vows!

Under the African tulip tree, corks pop. A crescent moon and a billion stars shine from the darkening sky as my childhood friend Lee walks to the microphone.

'On November 28, 1981, Gillian and Christo were married as the sun was setting ... Today family and friends celebrate and witness the reaffirmation of their vows ...'

Christo speaks first, turning to me as he finishes. 'You are the love of my life, my soul mate.'

My turn. But, just like twenty-five years ago, my voice catches when I try to speak. In happy tears, I stumble through the vows and fall into Christo's arms to loving applause.

Then Christo picks up his guitar and the crowd hushes. We step up to the mike, he strikes a chord and we start singing a toe-tapping Hank Williams song.

Comb your hair and paint and powder
With an excited howl Pablo breaks free of the rope that's been keeping him out of mischief.
You act proud and I'll act prouder
Charging straight for us, his lead catches under the p.a. amplifier and pulls it over.
You sing loud and I'll sing louder
Which only excites him more. Round and round us he runs, barking madly. Our guests go wild.
Tonight we're setting the woods on fire.

Bedlam and laughter whirl in the blustery wind as Christo picks away, flashing me that loving smile.

Beyond the pandemonium, I am half-aware of Alix wiping away a tear.

Me? In my new dress, with my husband at my side on our alp by the sea, I just keep on singing.

acknowledgments

This book comes from the heart, and I thank my loving husband Christo and my beautiful daughter Alix; my remarkable mother Norma; my green-fingered father Hec, who I miss; my sisters Janet and Kathleen, two very special women.

Thank you also to: Margot Foster for airing my radio anecdotes on the ABC's Bush Telegraph program; Hazel Flynn, commissioning editor for Murdoch Books, who heard one of the anecdotes, encouraged me to have a go at writing this book (despite my qualms) and became a friend in the process; Jacqueline Blanchard, who edited the manuscript and gently steered me through the deadlines; Lorrae Willox, who read the book painstakingly and rescued me from certain embarrassment, twice; Ian Baker, 'The Mentor', for consulting on gardening matters, including compost chemistry; neighbours and friends Nicky Smith and Geoff Goldrick, and Jim and Margaret Tedder, who all read the book and set me straight on matters of local geography, history, fauna and flora; environmentalist Michael Jones for his input on precious old-growth forest at Razorback Ridge; Brenna Gainge for her flattering photographs; Mr and Mrs S for their robust enthusiasm; Billie Crawford, of the Macleay River Historical Society, for a wealth of information. A Folk History of Yarrahapinni and Stuarts Point 1984 proved a useful resource.

(As this book was being completed, signage at the national park was changed from Yarrahapinni to Yarriabini to capture the Aborginal pronunciation more closely.)

First published in 2007 by Pier 9, an imprint of Murdoch Books Pty Limited

Murdoch Books Pty Limited Australia
Pier 8/9, 23 Hickson Road, Millers Point NSW 2000
Phone + 61 (0) 2 8220 2000 Fax + 61 (0) 2 8220 2558
Website: www.murdochbooks.com.au

Murdoch Books UK Limited
Erico House, 6th Floor, 93–99 Upper Richmond Road,
Putney, London SW15 2TG
Phone + 44 (0) 20 8785 5995 Fax + 44 (0) 20 8785 5985

Chief Executive: Juliet Rogers
Publisher: Kay Scarlett

Commissioning Editor: Hazel Flynn
Project Manager and Editor: Jacqueline Blanchard
Design Concept: Reuben Crossman
Designer: Sarah Odgers
Production: Adele Troeger
Cover photograph: Photolibrary

National Library of Australia Cataloguing-in-Publication Data:
Nicholson, Gillian Fiona, 1947– .
This way to the sea : the true story of a new life with an old love.
ISBN 9781740459655. ISBN 1 74045 965 2.
1. Nicholson, Gillian Fiona, 1947- . 2. Nicholson, Christo
(Christopher). 3. Banana growers - New South Wales -
Mid-North Coast - Biography. 4. Married people - New South
Wales - Mid-North Coast - Biography. I. Title. 634.772092

Printed by 1010 Printing International Limited. Printed in CHINA.
Text © Gillian Nicholson 2007.
Design © Murdoch Books Pty Limited 2007.